TAKING CHARGE OF YOUR LIFE

by Michael and Terri Quinn

HANDBOOK FOR THE YOUNG ADULT
ASSERTIVENESS PROGRAMME

FAMILY CARING TRUST

Copyright © Family Caring Trust, 1994
ISBN 1 872253 08 3

Illustrations and design: Pauline McGrath
Printing: Universities Press (Belfast)

All rights reserved. No part of this publication may be reduced, stored in a retrieval system, or transmitted, in any form or by any means, electronic, mechanical, photocopying, recording, or otherwise, without the prior permission of the publishers.

FAMILY CARING TRUST

IS PARTICULARLY GRATEFUL TO

FOR THEIR GENEROUS CONTRIBUTION

TOWARDS THE DEVELOPMENT AND PRODUCTION

OF THIS BOOK AND PROGRAMME

Acknowledgements

This book, and the programme of which it is a part, would have been impossible but for the co-operation we received from a great many people. We would like to thank Gabrielle and Julie Allman, Peter Devlin, David Gamble, Linda Irwin, Martin Kennedy, Philip Leonard, Dave Martin, Elizabeth McAllister, Catherine and Michael Molloy, Nuala Mulvenna, Colm O'Muiri, Keith Phipps, Katherine Tierney, and a great many young adults whose openness to experiencing the course and whose honest reactions to the book kept changing its shape throughout the different stages of piloting. Our special thanks also to Bernie Magill, our secretary, who was always willing to go the extra mile. And to our own children, two of whom (Ciaran and Veronica) made important contributions to the book.

CONTENTS

MY RIGHTS..7

BEFORE YOU BEGIN..8

CHAPTER ONE: WHAT ASSERTIVENESS MEANS......................9

CHAPTER TWO: SAYING 'NO'..18

CHAPTER THREE: DEALING WITH ABUSE AND CRITICISM....26

CHAPTER FOUR: WHEN YOU'RE ANNOYED OR ANGRY........35

CHAPTER FIVE: ENCOURAGEMENT AND ASSERTIVENESS....43

CHAPTER SIX: LISTENING..51

CHAPTER SEVEN: PROBLEMS!..60

CHAPTER EIGHT: A WAY OF LIFE...69

COMMENTS FROM YOUNG ADULTS.......................................78

GROUNDRULES..79

HERE ARE SOME OF MY RIGHTS:

1. I have a right to be treated with respect, no matter what my age is, or my sex or sexuality, or class, or race, or education, or work (paid or unpaid) - and regardless of any way in which I may be disabled.

2. I have a right to say 'no' - or 'yes', or 'I don't know', or 'I don't understand', or to say nothing at all.

3. I have a right to say what I feel.

4. I have a right to say what I think - and to change my mind and think differently in the future.

5. I have a right to state what I want or need or prefer, and to ask for it (though the answer may be 'no').

6. I have a right to postpone making a decision until I have time to think.

7. I have a right to be different from you in my feelings, ideas, wishes, needs, tastes, values, and standards.

8. I have a right to hear criticisms of my behaviour at first hand - rather than have others talk about me behind my back.

9. I have a right to make decisions that may not meet with the approval of others - even to make mistakes.

10. I have a right to question or confront any person or system or custom that oppresses others.

11. I have a right to be involved in decisions made by my family, my church or association, or a public body, when these decisions affect me.

12. I have a right to enjoy living.

With each of these rights there is a responsibility. For example, if I have a right to be treated with respect (number 1 above), I have a responsibility to treat others with respect; if I have a right to say 'no', or to say nothing (number 2 above), then I have a responsibility to respect other people's right to say 'no' or to say nothing. Form groups of three, start at number one, and see if you can answer these three questions in each case:
1. What's the responsibility corresponding to this right?
2. Do I think I have this right, and would I find it hard to claim?
3. Is it difficult for me to respect this right in other people?

BEFORE YOU BEGIN

The need for this book

Do you sometimes let others bully you, push you around, or ignore you, because you can't stand unpleasantness, rows or tension? And do you sometimes end up doing the same to others because that seems to be what's expected - and what gets results? If you do, cheer up - there are many others like you. But there may be a price to pay, both now and in later years.

The purpose of this book is to help you stand back and think about how you are living, and to introduce you to more assertive ways of behaving. You will find ideas here for getting along with people in ways which are more respectful and more effective, and which allow you to be become a more confident, encouraging, positive person. You will learn to stand up for yourself, deal with pressures, and take more control of your own life. You will also learn to enjoy living and to feel better about yourself.

Your own best teacher

You are your own best teacher. That is one of our beliefs in writing this book and in designing the programme of which it is a part. We believe that you learn best when you know what your own needs are rather than when someone else is telling you what you need to learn. You will be able to take control of your life more effectively when the thinking and the decisions, even the mistakes, are your own. There is value in learning from the ideas and experience of others - that is part of the process - but you are encouraged to react to any of the ideas in this book, to test them for yourself, to disagree, to think for yourself.

This flexibility applies to all the ideas here. Different people act assertively in different ways. When you come across a tip like: *'Look directly at the person'*, bear in mind that some people may be assertive when they choose *not* to look directly at the person they are speaking with. Similarly, if you have a teacher or parent who is intolerant and bossy, and you've decided it's pointless to do anything about them, that's okay; you can decide what's assertive for you. The guidelines in this book are only suggestions that may be worth trying. They are not rules.

Zoning in on family

Unlike much of the material for young adults, many of the examples here come out of a family context. This may surprise you, now that you are now beginning to *separate* from family and form new relationships. But it has a number of advantages.

Firstly, your family is a great place to practice these skills, because that is where most of us meet a lot of requests and demands and criticisms every day - and regular practice is the key to success in becoming more assertive.

There is a second reason for the emphasis on family. Many people believe that the way we treat our families today will be the way we will treat a partner in the future. If that is true, there may be lifelong benefits in improving the way we relate to those closest to us now.

Part of a course

This book is part of an eight-week, self-help course. It may be useful on its own, but the skills will be learnt more effectively when you read just one chapter a week (about three pages of text) and follow the programme in a small support-group of young adults. For those who wish to follow the course, a Leader's Guide and a video cassette are available separately from Family Caring Trust.

Whether you read the book or do the course linked with it, however, it is not realistic to expect to acquire these skills quickly. The book may give you a sense of direction, but skill and confidence will only come with practice. For that reason, you are strongly discouraged from making major decisions like changing career, leaving school, or tackling unfairness in a reactionary teacher or parent. It is better to start with small areas where you can get a sense of success and progress. Besides, as the course progresses, you will be learning skills like listening that help you to deal with conflict more effectively when you come to that stage. One of the principles of the course is to start small and move along only gradually. Good luck with that!

CHAPTER ONE: WHAT ASSERTIVENESS MEANS

Too 'nice' to protest

At seventeen years of age, Nicola Gibson is expected to make the sandwiches for her brother Richard's lunch - and to iron his shirts. Richard is nineteen. Nicola resents this, but she doesn't complain because she hates tension.

expected to make the sandwiches for her brother

When her mother wants to talk with Nicola, she bursts into her room without knocking. Nicola hates not having her privacy respected, but she never protests because she would hate to upset her mother.

Another thing that annoys her is her father's habit of changing channels without consulting her when they are both watching television. Moreover, when her father tells her to do something, he doesn't say 'please' or 'thank you', yet Nicola is so anxious to please him that she jumps to attention, and says, 'Yes, Dad.' She even tends to apologise when he shows anger or impatience, - even though she may not have done anything wrong.

Nicola's behaviour towards her family is passive and apologetic, and lacking in freedom. That's probably not good for *them*, in that they remain unaware of the effects of their behaviour. But it's not good for Nicola herself, because it prevents her from developing as a person. It prevents her from maturing and taking more control over her life.

This passive, apologetic approach is quite common when we are dealing with strangers or with those in authority. But let's see what happens when someone takes the *opposite* approach.

'No one walks on me!'

Patrick seems anything but passive and fearful. He is constantly at war with his brother and his parents. When asked a question, he often 'barks' an answer. He specialises in the Clint Eastwood look - the tough macho image with a sullen, angry glare, as if to say, 'No one walks on me!' He's right. No one walks on him. And when things aren't going his way, he blames, accuses, criticises, shouts, bangs doors, and throws tantrums. Everyone else is wrong! You can imagine what it's like to live with those bullying tactics. And you can imagine what kind of husband/ partner he may make one day if he continues with such aggressive behaviour. Like Nicola, Patrick has his own difficulty in becoming adult, but in quite a different way.

he often 'barks' an answer

Many people make the mistake of thinking that those who will not let themselves be walked upon are *assertive*. But acting aggressively should not be confused with acting assertively. Indeed, a good way to begin to understand assertiveness is to begin by understanding what it is *not*. We have just seen two common ways of behaving that are not assertive - behaving in a *passive* way; and behaving in an *aggressive* way. We'll look at them more closely now.

Let's say you're reading a magazine, but your younger sister is being a nuisance to you, continually seeking attention and not letting you concentrate. What do you do?

Passive behaviour

The passive response is to do little or nothing. You keep trying to read, making an occasional plea, or saying, 'Ah, now..' or 'Aw, please..' In the end, you may even give up what you are doing and give in to her demands.

People who act passively usually want to be 'nice'. So they bury many of their negative feelings in order to keep smiling. They mean well. Indeed, they often appear to have more respect for others than they have for themselves. But, like Nicola, in the first example above, they may be so afraid of tension that they will not claim their own rights or speak up for themselves. They can become doormats to others.

Many people act passively with their friends, neighbours and work mates. Because they are anxious to be liked, or to come across as 'reasonable', or because they are afraid of conflict or tension, they will often sacrifice their own rights. They will tend to agree with what others say, and they may find it difficult to say 'no' to extra demands. Anything for 'peace'. It's difficult for them to ask for or receive help. They may begin with

'I'm very sorry to bother you...'

something like, 'I'm very sorry to bother you..' They say 'sorry' a lot. Their body language is often apologetic too - a forced smile, hunched shoulders, lack of eye contact. They tend to bury their negative feelings in order to keep smiling - which may affect their health eventually. When they act like this, they are not respecting themselves.

Few people go as far as that, but a great many of us can probably identify with *some* of these behaviours or feelings. We may be quite assertive in some ways, but we may act passively in certain situations or with certain individuals. Some of us, for example, may act passively when we are with authority figures - a boss, a head teacher - or someone who seems to know a lot more than we do, like a doctor. And sometimes that may be okay - provided we are *choosing* to act in this way. But the passive behaviour we are talking about here is not assertive in so far as it is not free.

Aggressive behaviour

A second way of behaving that is not assertive (and is anything but passive); is the aggressive approach. You speak in frustration or anger to the younger sister who is annoying you, or you scold or threaten her, or you shout at her. You may even thump her. You say something like,

'Shut up, you little pest, and get out - now!'

trying to read a magazine

'Shut up, you little pest, and get out - now!'

With the passive approach, people do not respect themselves, but with the aggressive approach they show little or no respect for *others*. When they act aggressively, they often adopt a tough, hostile attitude and try to bully others into doing what they want. So they tend to use the word 'you' rather than 'I'. They'll say, 'You'd better..' or 'You should..' rather than 'I need..' or 'I'd like.' They *do* stand up for their rights, but they tend not to respect the rights of others - they will often antagonise and hurt others. They may be bluntly honest with you about your mistakes, but they usually won't notice your strengths, and they'll neglect to compliment you or to say something encouraging to you.

And you will notice, too, that people's body language will normally match this aggressive behaviour - the pointing finger, the angry, accusing eyes, the raised voice, the shouting or screaming, or the clenched fist.

It is interesting, too, that those who act passively and apologetically outside the home may be quite aggressive with their own families, or with those whom they take for granted.

A certain amount of aggression and anger may be okay - it's *normal* for those going through a difficult patch to blow their top from time to time. Any major change in life is scary, and when we feel scared or insecure, we're going to make mistakes as we try out different kinds of behaviour. But what we are talking about here is behaviour that is *constantly* aggressive - the *habit* of bullying, shouting, bossing, or making treats. There is nothing assertive about that.

Assertive behaviour

A third way of behaving is the assertive approach - an alternative to behaviour that is passive or aggressive. It is an approach that helps you to be direct, honest and respectful in expressing your wants, needs, opinions and feelings.

In the case above, an assertive approach might be to put the magazine down, look directly at your sister, and say, 'Sandra, I want to read this magazine, and I'm finding it difficult.' That may not be enough. You may have to negotiate with her, even to give in a bit and to give her some of the attention she's looking for. After all, **being assertive is not about winning or getting your own way - it's about respecting *both* yourself *and* others.**

Note, too, that the assertive reply does not say, 'Sandra, *I'm sorry*, but I want to...' If you have done something wrong, you say sorry, but you're not doing something wrong in claiming your rights. Saying sorry in a situation like this can put you into a passive, apologetic frame of mind.

the assertive approach

When people act assertively, their behaviour is neither apologetic nor aggressive, and they respect both their own rights and the rights of others. They are not afraid to say what they are thinking or feeling, or what they want or need or prefer. They will tend to use the word 'I' rather than 'you' ('I need..' or 'I prefer' rather than 'You need to..' or 'You just don't care!'). Whether they are making a request or dealing with criticism, they tend to look directly at you when they speak, and there is no apology in their tone of voice or posture. When they have to give a correction or stand up for someone's rights, or say 'no', or accept a compliment, they tend to face up to things, and you will notice that they can be quite at ease speaking directly and personally to you.

Few of us measure up to these high standards all the time. We are all assertive to some extent and in certain circumstances. Different people also act assertively in different ways. So there is no need to be bluntly honest in order to be assertive. It may be okay, for example, to be 'economical with the truth' in making an excuse. It may be better to tell someone that you are 'not free' to go down town with them rather than that you don't like them!

Three ways summed up

Here is an example of how you might deal with a situation in each of the three ways. It is a cold day, and you are travelling on a bus when someone asks you, 'Do you mind if I open a window?' You really do mind, because you're feeling extremely cold.

'Do you mind if I open a window?'

What might the *aggressive* response be? Something like a gruff, 'I certainly do mind! You fresh air fanatics think of nobody but yourselves!'

And the *passive* response? Perhaps, 'No, no, no - of course not. Please go ahead. I don't mind at all. I could do with some fresh air myself.'

And the *assertive* approach? You would probably avoid aggression by giving a direct, honest message. There is no 'right' way to express this - that will depend on the situation and on your own

'You fresh air fanatics...!'

personality, but you might say something like, 'Well, I'm feeling quite cold. I would really prefer you not to open it.'

Sometimes, you may have to talk things out and come to an arrangement that respects both of you. You may decide to agree to the window being *slightly* open, for example. Assertiveness calls us to be gentle and respectful and to avoid causing any unnecessary upset. You may dislike smoking in your presence, but in certain situations you may have your own good reasons for deciding to do nothing about it. In other words, you are making a choice and deciding what is assertive for you in that case. That is your right, and people would be wrong to judge you passive in a situation like that.

At the end of this chapter there is a table of five tips on being assertive, and in this book you will meet a number of different skills that enable you to treat yourself and others with respect in these ways. Respect is the key to assertiveness.

But my own way works!

A common objection to taking a more assertive approach is that the way you have been dealing with a situation has worked okay for a long time. Maybe you shout and bully a bit at home, but at least that seems to *work*.

There is a certain logic in this argument. The truth is that aggressive behaviour often *does* produce immediate results. But does that justify being disrespectful? And have you noticed that others tend to shout and lose their cool when you do? So it's a vicious circle. Aggression breeds aggression. Besides, how long does any positive effect last? Don't you end up having to shout and act tough to get the same effect again? Acting aggressively can all too easily become a lifetime habit.

It's sobering to think that at this moment you may be forming habits for life. Some people think

'Please go ahead! I don't mind at all...'

that there is a connection between the way you treat your brothers and sisters and parents at present and the way you are likely to treat your partner in the future. In other words, the kind of wife or husband you'll be may depend on how you treat those you live with right now.

A chance to take some control over our lives

Many young adults say they want to treat their future partners with more respect and love than they have experienced in their own families. That is something which learning to be more assertive offers. It offers us a chance to take some control over our lives, now and in the future, a chance to choose what we want to do with our lives and who we want to be with - and to be with them in a better way. It is an approach that enables us to communicate directly and openly and to act in a more relaxed and confident way, because it is founded on healthy self-respect and on respect for others.

TABLE 1: THREE WAYS OF BEHAVING

Below are three common ways of behaving. Which of these approaches do you tend to use?

APPROACH	ASSOCIATED WORDS	BODY LANGUAGE	EFFECT
AGGRESSIVE	Offensive, hostile, pushy, disrespectful, explosive, hurtful, putting down, rough, sarcastic, spiteful, angry, abusive, bossy, blaming.	Voice raised, pointing finger, glaring eyes, fist clenched...	Hurts people. Antagonises. Makes enemies. Others learn to be aggressive.
PASSIVE	Spiritless, oppressed, grin-and-bear-it, submissive, silent, miserable, sheepish, weak-kneed, over-anxious, held back, accommodating..	Apologetic tone, hands fidget, avoids eye contact, hunched shoulders..	Becomes a doormat. Is not respected Self-respect lessens. Allows others to be disrespectful.
ASSERTIVE	Positive, direct, free, steady, honest, just, relaxed, respectful, quiet, courageous, angry in healthy ways, personal, humorous, calm, peaceful, patient, encouraging, open.	Relaxed body posture, calm voice, steady eye contact...	Others feel respected. Self-esteem and self-confidence grow. Teaches others to respect.

TIPS ON BEHAVING ASSERTIVELY

Here are some tips on behaving assertively that have helped many people - though some of the examples may not be appropriate for your situation. Bear in mind that there is no such thing as an 'assertive person' - or an aggressive or passive person. Different people are assertive in different ways.

1. MAKE A HABIT OF SPEAKING **PERSONALLY**
   'I like that kind of music.' 'As an unemployed person I disagree with that.' 'I like you.' 'I think that's unfair.' 'I feel sad when you're too busy to sit down and listen.'

2. BE DIRECT IN LETTING OTHERS KNOW WHAT YOU WANT
   'I need a break.' 'I'd prefer to be on my own for an hour or so.' 'I don't want you to come this evening - that doesn't suit me.' 'I'd like a coke.' 'I'd like to travel with John.'

3. SAY WHAT YOU'RE **FEELING** - NOT JUST WHAT YOU'RE **THINKING**
   'I've had a late night, so I'm tired and in bad form.' 'This is going over my head - I'm feeling a bit lost - please explain it again.' 'When you speak to me like that, I feel confused - like a little boy in front of a cross teacher.' 'I'm impressed with the way you handled that.'

4. SPEAK **WITH** A PERSON - RATHER THAN **ABOUT** A PERSON
   'I had a sense that you were ignoring me, and that upset me.' 'That hurts me.' 'I'm feeling quite annoyed now, because I had asked you to stop doing that.'

5. ASK QUESTIONS, LISTEN, AND BE PREPARED TO MAKE SOME CHANGES - INSTEAD OF ARGUING OR GOING ON THE DEFENSIVE.
   'I wonder why you said that?' 'Can you tell me a bit more?' 'That's how I see it, but I know you see it differently - how do <u>you</u> feel about it?' 'Tell me what you think would make you happier.' 'No, I'm not prepared to be the only one doing chores in the kitchen - but I <u>am</u> prepared to be fair and play my part.'

CASE STUDIES

Form groups of three and talk about what you think someone might say or do in the following situations if they were: a) aggressive b) passive c) assertive:

1. You are travelling by bus, and feeling cold, when someone asks, 'Do you mind if I open a window?' Example:

<u>Aggressive:</u> 'Of course I do. It's freezing! You fresh air fanatics only think of yourselves!'

<u>Passive:</u> 'No, no, no - of course not. Please go ahead. I don't mind at all!'

<u>Assertive:</u> 'Yes, I'm feeling quite cold. I'd prefer you not to open it.' (Or you might agree to the window being opened slightly.)

2. You are so glad to have a part-time job that you've accepted low wages. Now you've been told you'll be expected to work longer hours without any extra pay. (Aggressive: Passive: Assertive:)

3. Your mother nags at you a lot but makes excuses for your brother (who is her favourite). (Aggressive: Passive: Assertive:)

4. Your boy friend says you're so old-fashioned he can hardly believe it - everybody has sex nowadays. (Aggressive: Passive: Assertive:)

5. You are watching television; your father comes and changes channels without consulting you. (Aggressive: Passive: Assertive:

6. Your friend comes around to your house almost every day and stays for hours. You understand that this friend is lonely, but you feel a bit trapped. (Aggressive: Passive: Assertive:)

7. You 'fancy' someone but feel extremely nervous about telling her/him. (Aggressive: Passive: Assertive:)

8. Your friend arranged to meet you down town and turns up over twenty minutes late - as usual. (Aggressive: Passive: Assertive:)

Can you think of other examples?...

SKILL PRACTICE

1. For the Skill Practice you are asked to form pairs. Here are some assertive statements, but it is quite possible to say them aggressively (angry face, shouting, possibly with finger pointing) or passively (shoulders hunched, apologetic voice, not looking at the person.)

Take turns with your partner in saying them aggressively, then passively, and then assertively:

'I like that kind of music'/ 'I think that's not fair'/ 'Look, I feel sad when you're too busy to sit down and listen'/ 'I need a break'/ 'I don't want you to come this evening - that doesn't suit me'/ 'I've had a late night and I'm tired and in bad form'/ 'How do <u>you</u> feel about it?'/ 'That's how I see it.'

2. Next, if you have time, you could take turns in dealing *assertively* with *any* of the situations in the Case Studies section. Use some of the approaches suggested in the Tips (above), if you like, but get some feedback each time on how you're coming across. Maybe your tone of voice is too apologetic or too aggressive. If so, you may need to try it again until you get it right. You might take turns, one of you attempting to be assertive in one situation, and then the other in a different situation. Or you may like to try being assertive in a real life situation that you normally find difficult.

PLANNING FOR NEXT WEEK

Please read *chapter two* for next week - it helps a lot to have the chapter read before each session.

Tick any of the following people with whom you would <u>like</u> to be more assertive: A demanding sister or brother; a bossy parent, step-parent or guardian; a friend who is a bit insensitive; a teacher, employer or other authority figure; a friend who never seems to be able to make up his/her mind; someone you know who does not treat you with respect; a nosey neighbour; a local bully; an interfering relative..

Pick one or two situations where you will be less aggressive, less passive, more assertive in the coming week (not big ones - it is important to go for small manageable ones for a start; that will give you the confidence to tackle bigger issues later). Then plan as specifically as possible what approach you will take, where, when, who with, etc.

Who will I be more assertive with? In what situation? What will I do?

Plans... _____

_____

CHAPTER TWO: SAYING 'NO'

'No problem at all!'

'Barry, will you stay on this evening?'

It was Mrs Thomas who spoke. She was the supervisor in the local supermarket where Barry had a part-time job, and he liked to be on good terms with her - but he had a date for that evening.

'Er.. This evening?' Barry stammered, taken aback.

'Yes, we need an extra pair of hands.'

'Okay.. How long will you need me, Mrs Thomas?'

He hoped she might say that an hour would be sufficient, or even an hour and a half. That way, he could just about manage to keep his date.

'About three hours.' she answered, 'All right?'

'No problem,' he said.

As soon as she had left, Barry could have kicked himself for being so weak.

'There I go again.' he thought to himself, 'I'm my own worst enemy. Why can't I say "no" to people like Mrs Thomas? And why do I say "no problem"! Why am I so *willing*!'

Barry finds it hard to say 'no'. It is nice to meet people who are willing and co-operative, but Barry is not acting out of a spirit of co-operation when he is merely taking the line of least resistance. This is passive behaviour, and it is not uncommon with people in authority.

'I'm my own worst enemy!' he thought

Meeting pressures and demands

So what can you do? How do you begin to cope with the enormous pressures young adults have to face today to conform, to do what everyone else in your group does, to wear the same clothes, to live the same lifestyle, sometimes to drink too much, to experiment with drugs, to go all the way in sex... How do you say 'no' respectfully and yet firmly when you need to?

In Table 2, at the end of this chapter, you can see a number of different ways of dealing assertively with pressures and demands. It is suggested that you begin by asking questions and finding out more about whatever it is you are being asked to do. Remember that you always have the right to ask for time to think. If you then decide that you need to say 'no', give your honest reasons, and say 'no' firmly but without aggression. It is important to *use* the word 'no'. Watch your tone of voice and body language. Sometimes a 'no' is not firm because you are apologising or explaining too much, or because you're giving a double message - smiling and trying to look sweet in the hope that you'll still be liked.

'Broken record'

If your 'no' is *not* being respected, that is, if the other person continues to be pushy, even rude, you may like to consider using the 'broken record' method. This means repeating the same sentence

'No problem!' he said

again and again, without any further explanations or excuses, 'No, it doesn't suit me... Yes, I'm sure I do sound mean, but it doesn't suit me... I don't think you've heard me - it doesn't suit me...'

This may feel disrespectful or impolite. You may be tempted to be 'reasonable' and offer explanations. But remember that this approach is *only* used with those who are being rude or 'pushy' with you. The truth is that if you give reasons or explanations to someone who is badgering you or treating you disrespectfully, they will often use them against you to hook you into further arguments or discussion - and may then push you into doing exactly what they want. Do you know that some salespeople are *trained* to catch you out on your excuses and reasons? Once you say something like, 'Maybe later' they may have caught you - 'Okay, could we say next week?' Or if you say, 'I'm sorry. I haven't enough money at present', again they may have caught you - 'Don't worry, we provide the finance.' So 'broken record' may be a useful skill to have.

This kind of repetition is essentially a respectful approach. As you repeat your phrase, you show respect by letting the other person know that you hear what they are saying. This will become clearer if we look at some examples of how to deal with requests and demands.

When you're not sure...

We'll begin by looking at how you might deal with a request when you are not sure whether the answer will be 'yes' or 'no'.

'Can I come back to you in an hour?'

Mother: 'Oh, Debbie, I'm glad you're home. Angela's here. She was looking for you.'
Debbie: 'Hi, Angela. You were looking for me?'
Angela: 'Yes. I'd like you to baby-sit for me tomorrow evening.'
Debbie: 'What time?'
Angela: 'Eight - until eleven or twelve.'
Debbie: 'Oh, I'm not sure, Angela. Can I come back to you in an hour when I've talked with Jenny? I think we've something on.'

An hour later, Debbie was back.
Debbie: 'Angela, Jenny and I are working together on our project tomorrow evening, but I'm happy to baby-sit if she can come along with me...'

This is an example of how a request can be dealt with. For ordinary small requests, of course, you will naturally make decisions on the spot - when you're asked to close the door, you don't need to ask for time to think about it. For bigger decisions, however, you can always ask for time. Notice that Debbie didn't say an immediate 'yes' or 'no'; she began by asking questions and finding out what was involved. She needed time, so she asked for it. And when she came back to Angela, she showed a willingness to negotiate. Making decisions often calls for some negotiation.

A reasonable 'no'

Now let's take it a step further and look at an example of someone saying *'no'* to a request.

Diane Chapman is a single parent who does not want to 'let go' of her eighteen year old son, David. She is terrified that he may no longer need her and may now want to live his own life. So she tends to be clingy and over-possessive of him. Visiting relatives on Sunday afternoons has become one of the battlefields in this tension. David hates these visits. His mother has just asked him to come with her to visit her sister.

'No, Mum,' he said, 'I don't want to go. I find it very boring. I know you two love your chat, but I sit there feeling really fed up. I hate it.'

'But it won't be the same without you, David..' His mother looked disappointed.

David felt torn. It was difficult for him to make a stand, because he hated to disappoint his mother. But he also knew that he needed to respect *himself* as well. He felt like replying that she didn't even notice him when she was visiting, but he knew it wouldn't help to argue. Better to speak personally.

'Mum, I hate to disappoint you, and I'm not saying that I'll never again go visiting with you on Sundays, but I hate those visits. I find them totally boring, and I don't want to go today.'

'Oh, you're impossible!'

'I see. You're glad of me when you need your clothes washed and your dinner cooked, but you don't want to be seen out with me any more.'

This was unfair, particularly since David co-operated quite a bit with the household chores. But he avoided getting hooked into an argument. Using 'broken record' is a better approach when someone is being disrespectful or unfair to you.

'I have no problem being seen out with you, but I don't want to go today.'

'So that's it then. Just as cold as that!'

'I'm sure it may seem cold, mum, but I don't want to go.'

'Oh, you're impossible!' And she stormed off.

When she hadn't got her own way, Diane had attempted to manipulate David with guilt. And he *did* feel guilty. Saying 'no' was difficult for him, but he was learning to turn a deaf ear to that kind of unnecessary guilt.

When you're not being respected

This is an example of a 'reasonable no' - with some use of the 'broken record' technique when that became necessary towards the end. All of us have to say 'no' from time to time, and David did so gently but firmly. Note that he spoke personally and gave his reasons for not wanting to go visiting. His mother then began to use emotional arguments. David remained calm, and fixed on one simple sentence, 'I don't want to go.' Instead of repeating this phrase over and over, however, he also continued to show that he was listening and was hearing what his mother was saying. That respectful approach is part and parcel of the 'broken record' method - using this method need never be an excuse for being aggressive or disrespectful.

What makes 'broken record' so powerful is that those on the receiving end of it quickly get the message that they are up against a stone wall and that you are not going to change your mind. It is also fairly easy to use, because you repeat the same phrase no matter what arguments or abuse the other person uses. If you do hear something new, however, it is important to stop repeating your 'no', to ask a question, and to show that you really are open to listening. 'Broken record' should only be used in situations where your rights are not being respected.

We'll look now at another example of 'broken record', for it is a useful method in the hands of anyone who is being badgered, disrespected or put under a lot of pressure (and young adults today tend to meet more than their share of pressures).

'A little drink won't hurt you.'

When Sandy Leonard decided, one Saturday evening, that he had had enough to drink, his friends became quite intolerant and began to coax and badger him to keep drinking.

'Come on, another pint won't hurt you..'

'No, thanks, I still have this one to drink. I've had enough.'

'Aw, what kind of a man are you! Can you not hold your drink like the rest?'

That got to Sandy a bit, especially coming from his friend, Graham, and he squirmed inside. He began to feel as if he was just being odd. But he stayed with his 'broken record' phrase, looked directly at Graham and said:

'I said I've had enough.'

'Ah, come on, Sandy! You're going to have another. Just one more pint..'

Sandy kept eye-contact with Graham, though he did not feel as calm as he looked.

'No', he said, 'I'm not going to have another one. I've had enough, thanks.'

'A little drink won't hurt you!'

'Well I'm getting you another one, whether you want it or not.'

'You can get another one if you like, but I'm not drinking it. I've had enough.'

'But that's crazy, man.'

'It *may* seem crazy to you, but I've had enough to drink.'

'Look, we're all looking forward to having a good time and you're spoiling the fun by not drinking.'

'*I'm* having fun - but I've had enough to drink.'

'Some fun! Seriously, Sandy, you're pissing me off! Have another pint with the rest of us!'

'Graham, I don't think you've heard me. I've had enough to drink.'

People can be quite intolerant of someone who is 'different', who does not think and act as the rest of their group does. Yet Sandy's is quite a simple technique. He doesn't have to think up clever things to say. He doesn't have to make excuses. He makes no apologies. He just stays with the same sentence, acknowledging each time that he has heard what his friend is saying to him.

'Everybody has sex nowadays!'

We'll look now at a final example in which a young woman is being pressurised by her boyfriend to have sex. She has already told him why she doesn't want to sleep with him, but he continues to pressurise her, so 'broken record' is appropriate.

'Come on, Allison, it's not as if we're strangers. We've been seeing each other for weeks.'

Here he goes again, Allison thought. He really doesn't respect me when he keeps pressurising me like this.

'No, Neil', she said, 'I've told you I don't want to sleep with you, and I've given you my reasons. Now why don't you respect me?'

'But I don't get it. What's the big deal? Everybody has sex nowadays.'

'Not me', she said, and then, fixing on her 'broken record' phrase, she repeated, 'I don't want to sleep with you.'

'But you said you liked me and trusted me...'

'I do, but I don't want to sleep with you.'

'Oh, loosen up a bit. Sex is fun. You'll really enjoy it.'

'I'm sure you're right, but I don't want to sleep with you'

'But what are you afraid of? I have a condom. You're not going to get hurt.'

'I know you wouldn't want to hurt me - but I don't want to sleep with you.'

'But there's no point saying no to something you haven't tried. Why don't we just try it once and then make up our minds about continuing?'

'No, I'm not comfortable with that - I don't want to sleep with you.'

'I don't believe it. You're so stubborn! Why do we go on seeing each other if we can't express ourselves?'

Who's the stubborn one! Allison thought, but she didn't allow herself to get side-tracked from using 'broken record'.

'I'd like to go on seeing you because I want to get to know you, Neil, but I don't want to sleep with you.'

The rewards

You notice here that Allison remained polite. By using 'broken record' she was able to remain firm without being either apologetic or aggressive. She didn't say, 'I don't want to sleep with you *now*', for example, for that would have let him get a foot in the door (opening the way to, '*When* can we have sex then?') Nor did she blindly repeat the same sentence - she showed that she was listening, hearing what Neil was saying. Using this skill well enabled her to respect herself and Neil at the same time.

Saying 'no' takes courage as well as skill. It may *cost* you something. You may even lose some friends. It takes considerable will-power to continue to say 'no' in the face of today's pressures. But standing up for yourself builds *character* and helps you grow in maturity.

Saying 'no' to limits?

That doesn't mean saying 'no' to sharing the household chores or to your parents' limits. Question their limits by all means. Talk them out, and insist on limits that are fair to *everyone*. If your parents

'Everybody has sex nowadays!'

don't want to know, go back to them again and again until they respect your right to be heard and to have a say in the decisions that affect you. But other people have rights too. If you live at home, for example, it's only reasonable that you do your fair share of the household chores. Even if you have partly left home, it's hardly fair to arrive for weekends and expect a parent to prepare all your meals, to clean up after you, to do your laundry and be your servant. Where is the respect there - for yourself or for your parent? What kind of life and future relationships will you have if you act like that, if you want 'freedom' without limits? Assertiveness is always fair, always respectful of self and others.

Summing up

To sum up, then. Some people, have difficulty in saying 'no'. One simple approach is:

1. You ask questions.

2. If necessary, you ask for time to think.

3. You say a clear 'yes' or 'no', stating your reasons - but negotiating if necessary.

This might be the *normal* response to requests. The 'broken record' approach should only be used if you are not being respected. That means stating your position and calmly repeating it again and again. With practice, you can be firm, gentle, more assertive and more confident in dealing with the many requests and demands you meet.

TABLE 2: IF YOU HAVE TO SAY 'NO'

When someone comes to you with a request or a demand, it is good to begin by asking questions - and, if necessary, asking for time to think. If you have to say 'no', this table shows two ways of doing so without being aggressive or apologetic. The second way should only be used when you are being badgered, or when your 'no' is not being respected.

STAGE 1: A REASONABLE 'NO'

SAY 'NO' POLITELY AND FIRMLY (WATCH YOUR BODY LANGUAGE)

No, I don't want another vodka because..

No, I'd prefer not to go out with you, thanks.

SAY WHY CLEARLY - GIVE YOUR REAL REASONS, NOT 'EXCUSES'

I find any more goes to my head..

..because I don't want to get involved with anyone at the moment...

DON'T REJECT THE PERSON - AND BE OPEN TO ALTERNATIVES

..but I'd like an apple juice instead.

..but I'd like to stay friends with you.

STAGE 2: BROKEN RECORD 'NO'

KEEP REPEATING YOUR 'NO'

I don't want another vodka.. No, thank you, I don't want another one.

No, I don't want to go out with you. .. Yes, I do like you, but I don't want to go out with you.

KEEP LISTENING AND REMAIN POLITE
(Body language matching - steady eye contact, calm voice, good posture, stay friendly)

Yes, I hear what you're saying, but I don't want another one... Yes, I'm sure that does disappoint you, but I don't want another one.

Yes, I'm sure it is difficult for you, but I don't want to go out with you.. Maybe that does seem cold, but I don't want to go out with you.

BUT GIVE NO FURTHER EXPLANATIONS - JUST REPEAT SAME PHRASE

I don't think you heard me - I don't want another vodka.

Thanks for asking me, but I don't want to go out with you.

GETTING IN TOUCH

Tick any of these reasons why you find it difficult to say 'no' - even sometimes. Then underline the reason that seems to most prevent you from being assertive in saying 'no'.

- I'm afraid of hurting the other person, so I go along with them.
- I'm afraid of the other person's anger.
- I'm afraid of not being liked.
- I feel under pressure from my friends.
- It's easier to give in and do what someone else expects.
- I lose my nerve when I meet people in authority, so I say 'yes'.
- I haven't enough will-power to say 'no'.
- I think it's the right thing to do to be agreeable and say 'yes'.
- I find it hard to make decisions so it's easier to say 'yes'.
- It makes me feel guilty and uncomfortable to say 'no'.
- I upset plans and I'm a nuisance if I say 'no'.
- It feels disrespectful to say 'no' without making excuses.
- Another reason........

Take a few minutes to share your answers with the person beside you. Can you think of a time when you wanted to say 'no' but didn't:

CASE STUDIES

Mark each of the following situations with an 'R' (for a Reasonable 'No' - the first approach in Table 2), or with a 'BR' (for a Broken Record 'No' - the second approach in Table 2), depending on which approach you think might be most suitable. Then, in groups of three, take a few minutes to chat about why you marked each one as you did. Respect the point of view of anyone who differs from you.

1. A friend, whose feelings you don't want to hurt, has asked you out, but you don't feel attracted to her/him. (R or BR?)
2. Your parents expect you to come with them every time they go to visit relatives.
3. Your friends are using a lot of arguments to convince you to smoke dope with them.
4. Your older brother, whom you're afraid of, is putting pressure on you to give him money.
5. Your friend is pressurising you to have sex, and is trying to wear you down.
6. Your friends want you to come with them to a concert which you really can't afford.
7. Someone at your door is collecting for a 'Charity' or organisation you don't really want to support.
8. A man whom you don't know has offered you a lift home in his car. He won't take 'no' for an answer.
9. Your friend is very persuasive that you go down town with her/him - at a time when you have a lot of work to catch up on.
10. A teacher (or employer) asks you to stay late to help tidy up, but you have a date for that evening.
11. Your sister is pestering you to buy her sweets.
12. You have bought an old car and are out with your friends. They want you to drive faster - to 'push it over a hundred'.

SKILL PRACTICE

1. For the Skill Practice you are asked to form groups of three. Here are some assertive statements, but they can be said aggressively (with angry face, shouting, possibly with finger pointing, etc.) or passively (with shoulders hunched, speaking awkwardly, apologetic eyes, etc.)

Take turns in saying them, one at a time, aggressively, then passively, and then assertively:

'What do you mean by that?'/ 'When you speak to me like that, I feel hurt./ 'I don't like that word'/ 'How do you feel about it?'/ 'That's how I see it.'/ 'I need some money now.'/ 'What's wrong with you?'/ 'No, I'm not happy about that.'/ 'No. I don't want another one.'/ 'No, that doesn't suit me'/ 'No, I don't want to go with you.'

2. Next, still in your group of three, practise the 'broken record' method. Choose any one of the 'Case Study' situations which you marked BR - or, better still, a suitable example from your own life. One of you will act assertively, beginning politely by giving reasons, but then using 'broken record'; the second person will be the one who is badgering or pressurising; and the third will be the 'observer'. Each time, stop after a minute, the 'assertive' person comments on how they think they got on, and then the observer comments about:

Posture - comfortable, hunched, apologetic?..
Eye-contact - direct, open, glaring, steady?..
Face expression - cross, relaxed?..
Tone of voice - harsh, gentle, raised, calm, angry?..
Overall - polite and respectful, but firm?..

You're asked to do this exercise three times, with three different situations, but changing roles each time - each person will have a chance to act assertively, to be the one making the request, and to be the observer.

PLANNING FOR NEXT WEEK

Please read chapter three for next week - it is a great help to have the chapter read before each session.

Over the next week, take special care with your body language and tone of voice.

1. When are you likely to find it difficult to say 'no'? Or when will you need to be assertive in general? How will you deal with that?... Make some plans - and then feel free to talk them out with the person beside you.

2. It is also suggested that you take time *each evening* to relax your body and mind, become aware of how assertive you have been, and then foresee how you will act in one situation you'll be meeting the following day. See yourself acting assertively - keeping self-control but staying friendly. The more vividly you see it all, the more likely you are to be assertive. You may have to do this for a number of days before you see a difference in how you behave, but this daily exercise can have a powerful effect in helping you make these skills your own in a natural way. Such awareness can be the key to effective change.

When will I take time each day to become aware and to foresee my behaviour?

*Plans...*_____

_____

CHAPTER THREE: DEALING WITH ABUSE AND CRITICISM

they begin to believe they're stupid

Life is pretty rough for some people. Occasionally you'll even meet young girls and boys who already look a bit defeated. And you can understand it. If someone is constantly scolded and bossed and nagged at, they begin to believe the hurtful things that are said to them - that they are useless and stupid, that they don't care, that they can't be trusted, that they're nuisances. They may then accept the abuse passively, they cringe before those in authority, they become 'victims', they may even marry abusive people, and they become a shadow of what they could be and what they are meant to be.

Abuse is not always obvious. Sometimes there may be no words spoken at all. It may be a dirty look - or the fact that you're ignored, or interrupted, or laughed at, or overlooked. The words used may be perfectly harmless, but they are said with sarcasm or aggression - or in a patronising, superior tone of voice - and you know you're being put down. Or rather, you *allow* yourself to be put down. For, as you'll see, you *do* have a choice.

Aggressive reactions to abuse

It is noticeable that people who act in passive, apologetic ways at school or at work, with their friends or with relatives, will often be aggressive with their families. Far from accepting criticism or abuse passively at home, they can feel free to lash out and give as good as they get. That may be better than smiling and bottling up feelings - but meeting abuse with abuse can be destructive to themselves and to their families and to others. Let's see that for ourselves.

Alec's mother is in a bad mood and is finding fault with everything since she got up this morning. Alec had asked her if he could go to a football match that afternoon, and she had said 'no'. When he pleaded with her, she turned on him angrily.

'Look', she said, 'Would you shut up! I'm tired of you going on and on. You're a pain!'

Alec looked annoyed.

'You're a pain yourself!' he said, grumpily.

'Now don't you start giving me cheek!'

'Look who's talking about giving cheek. You started it. It was you called me a pain first!'

'And you are a pain. Just go away now and stop hanging around the kitchen and holding me back! Go to some other room and don't be such a nuisance!'

Mad with his mother, and determined not to let her think she had won, Alec fired his parting shot as he left the kitchen.

'Bitch!' he said.

Losing the real battle

Look at what happened here. Alec reacted to his mother's abuse by fighting back. You could hardly blame him; that's what most people do, and he probably didn't even know he had an alternative. So he met abuse with abuse. Not once did he use the word 'I' or say how he felt. Instead of an 'I-message', he used 'you-messages' ('You're a pain yourself!', 'You started it!') It is a common mistake to fight back at people with the word 'you' - 'You're not so hot yourself!' 'You don't know what you're talking about!' 'You're one to talk!'

Another mistake was not to ask a question. As so often happens, there was no listening on either side, no respect, only blind arguing and a determination to 'win'. But what do you win by being aggressive? Not respect. A certain amount of anger can be a healthy thing, but once you stop listening and become blindly aggressive, you begin to lose both your own self-respect and the respect of the other person. When you become aggressive, you generally lose the real battle.

Asking questions

Neither the aggressive approach, then, nor the passive one, is an assertive - or helpful - way to deal with abuse. So what is the assertive approach? How do you meet criticism and abuse in a way that allows you to keep your dignity and self-respect?

Every situation is different, so there is no one approach that applies across the board. But one effective way of dealing with abuse is to ask a direct question. 'Why did you say that?' 'What do you mean by...?' Let's go back to the example of Alec and his mother. Remember how she put him down:

'Look, would you shut up! I'm tired of you going on and on. You're a pain!'

Now let's listen to Alec dealing with the situation assertively.

'Mum, hold on a minute, why are you shouting at me?'

'I'm not shouting', she said, in a quieter voice.

'Why do you say I'm a pain?' he asked.

'Because you are a pain!'

'It hurts when you call me names like that.'

'Oh, don't be silly!'

'I don't call you names. Why do you feel you need to call me names? I hate you treating me like this.'

'Look, would you go off and give me peace!' his mother snapped.

'Mum, have you heard what I said? It hurts when you call me names. I hate you treating me like this.'

'Then stop pestering me!'

'How am I pestering you?'

'You're moaning on and on about going to the match.'

'I did ask you to think about it again. I don't think that's moaning, is it?'

'Oh, give over. I'm too busy to argue with you.'

The value of questions

In this case, Alec's mother continued to be abusive. Many young adults have to live with a good deal of disrespect and abuse. It's not surprising that they often hit back and say equally hurtful and disrespectful things. But all it takes is for one person to refuse to be sucked into the bickering, to choose instead to be assertive. That is what Alec had done.

It may appear that he wasn't successful in asserting himself, as his mother kept up the hostile front. But **being assertive does not guarantee that you will win, or that the other person will change. Being assertive is not about winning or getting your own way.** The goal is to keep your dignity, refusing to let yourself be put down by the disrespect you experience. To make this point more clearly, we have deliberately chosen an example of assertiveness here where the person acting assertively did *not* 'win'.

And yet, Alec's questions were not just good for himself, helping him to keep his dignity and self-respect. They were also good for his mother. For his questions were getting to her, forcing her to become aware of how she was treating him. As it happens, she was anxious to save face, and not in a mood to say she was sorry, but Alec was giving her something to think about, and she probably felt uncomfortable by the end of their encounter. This often happens when you confront an abuser with direct questions. You help them to think about what they are saying.

'Levelling' with people

The other assertive thing which Alec did was to speak personally ('It hurts when you call me names like that.' 'I don't call you names.' 'I hate you treating me like this.') This openness - using the word 'I', saying what's going on for you and how you feel - is often called 'levelling', because it helps you and the other person to be more equal, more on a level. It may also stop the other person in their tracks, and make them think, when you say something like, 'I feel hurt by what you've just said', or, 'I don't like you joking about that. It upsets me.' (But it is not appropriate to be so open with everyone - with some people your trust could be abused.)

We'll look at another example of how someone might deal with abuse, this time with more emphasis on using 'I-messages' than on asking questions - for your approach will depend a lot on the circumstances.

Katy dresses quite well, but she dislikes a popular new fashion and has just had the courage (or assertiveness) to say so in a group of her schoolmates. One of the group, who dislikes Katy, looks at her and sneers:

'What would you know about fashion! Look at how *you* dress!'

'Mum, what do you mean by that?'

'Excuse me?' Katy said, 'What did you say?'

That was a good start. It may help to get someone to repeat an abusive remark. Her friend was a little less confident this time as she repeated,

'I said - look at how you dress!'

Katy resisted the temptation to make a hurtful remark in return. She stayed with asking questions.

'And what's wrong with the way I dress?'

'It's crap!' Anne said.

She was obviously being deliberately abusive. Katy decided to use an 'I-message', to speak personally. She looked directly at Anne as she spoke. There was no apology in her voice. She said simply, 'I like the way I dress.'

'I like the way I dress.'

'Excuse me?...'

Abusers have to 'win'. The last thing they want is for someone to 'level' with them or to talk personally.

'Huh!' came the reply.

Katy didn't flinch:

'You may not like the way I dress, but I like it.'

'Oh, shut up!' Anne said.

Katy kept eye-contact, and came back with another 'I- message'.

'Anne, I don't like being treated like this.'

'Oh, bugger off!'

'I don't like that either.'

'I don't care what you like!'

'Maybe you don't - but I still don't like it.'

'I'll talk to you any way I want.'

'I'm sure you will. But I don't like it.'

The advantages of being honest with people

Talking personally is quite a powerful way of dealing with abuse. When that does not stop the abuse, you may then have to fix on a personal statement to repeat, 'broken record' fashion, as Katy did above. That is a simple, effective way to deal with abuse. You gradually wear down your abuser, because, no matter what they say, you are never left speechless, yet you are neither passive nor aggressive - provided you watch your body language.

There is another great advantage in being honest with people in this way, using the word 'I' and 'levelling' with them. Your openness will often help them to think about how they are acting. Eventually, they may even open up and become more honest with you, perhaps expressing some of their own frustration, anger and pain. For when others blame, criticise or abuse you, it's good to remember that they may be quite hurt themselves. Or they may be annoyed about something completely different, something that has nothing to do with you.

'Your work is not up to standard'

We have looked now at the two chief skills for dealing with criticism - asking questions ('what's wrong with the way I dress?') and speaking personally ('That's abuse. I don't like it.') But the examples so far have been of criticism that was destructive. In fact, criticism may be quite *constructive*, and is not at all a bad thing. None of us *likes* to be criticised, but it is *essential* for us to get constructive criticism if we are to improve. Again, asking a question instead of reacting in anger is an assertive way to begin to deal with it, for that shows your openness to listening and to changing. Let's look at an example.

'Your work is just not up to standard.'

Mr Mullan is the supervisor in a mail order firm. He has just sent for Yvonne, one of the young packers.

'This isn't good enough, Miss Spencer, your work is just not up to standard.'

'Why do you say that?' Yvonne asked.

'I've had three complaints from customers in the last week. When their orders were supplied, all three of them found that there was something missing or incorrect.'

> **If you are the victim of serious physical or sexual abuse, it may not be appropriate at all to attempt to be assertive with the person directly involved. It will be more important to be assertive in contacting your local social services or telling someone who will take you seriously and will do something about it.**

'Mm. That's not good. Will you give me the details and I'll check them out.'

Half an hour later, she was back.

'One of the complaints was my mistake,' she said. 'I'm sorry. I normally double-check each order I make up, and I didn't double-check that batch because I was under pressure. The other two orders weren't handled by me. You remember I wasn't here on Tuesday.'

'I see. You know *all* orders have to be double-checked, Yvonne. Pressure of work is no excuse. How are you going to prevent this happening in future?'

'Well, if I'm under pressure, I'll have to shout and make sure I have extra help, or else we'll have to leave some orders till the following day.'

'Okay. That would be better than making them up incorrectly under pressure.'

Yvonne looked directly at Mr Mullan as she spoke her next sentence.

'There is something I want to say, Mr Mullan. I was a bit shocked this morning when you said my work was unsatisfactory. I wonder if that was fair?..'

Ways of dealing with criticism

In this situation, we see that Yvonne began with a certain basic openness. Instead of becoming defensive or going on the attack, as so often happens in such circumstances, she asked a question. She wanted details.

Secondly, she knew that one of her rights was the right to have some time to think - time to consider the criticism and check it out. She did that.

Thirdly, she came back to the supervisor, took responsibility for her own mistake, and showed herself open to making some changes. But there was nothing slavish in her approach - indeed, she made a strong 'I-statement', making it clear she had no intention of allowing herself to be put down. She had handled the criticism assertively - with openness and self-respect.

To sum up then. Unless a person is upset or in pain, it is suggested that you begin dealing with criticism by asking questions. If the person continues to be critical and even abusive, you can then make a personal statement - and go on repeating it as long as the abuser continues to put you down. If the criticism may be true, however, you may want to take some time to think about it or check it out. Then you firmly accept or reject it. And finally, you talk out any changes that you may now need to make.

Other ways of standing up for yourself

As well as asking questions and making personal statements, there are a number of other ways of dealing with abuse or unfair criticism. One obvious thing is simply to steer clear of those who abuse

'There is something I want to say, Mr Mullan..'

'Mm.. Could be right...'

you, if that is possible. Indeed, if you are the victim of serious physical or sexual abuse, it may not be appropriate at all to attempt to be assertive with the person directly involved. It will be more important to be assertive in contacting your local social services or telling someone who will take you seriously and will do something about it.

Another way of dealing with abuse is to use 'fogging'. Quite simply, this means dealing with someone who is abusive (for example, a sister or brother who constantly wants to argue and prove you wrong) by saying, 'Mm.. Could be,' or, 'You've a point there,' or, 'Maybe you're right.' The attacker then doesn't know where they stand; you haven't agreed with them, but you haven't disagreed, and it's impossible to fight with an enemy who has just disappeared into the fog. For that is what you do with this method - disappear into a fog without losing face. Hence the expression 'fogging'. (Joking may be another form of 'fogging' - but not sarcastic 'joking'.)

As we saw, 'broken record' may also be a useful way of dealing with those who criticise you unfairly. You deny the criticism clearly and firmly and fix on a phrase that you continue to repeat, 'That is abuse, and I won't let you abuse me.' 'Yes, I accept that you didn't mean it that way, but it's abuse, and I won't let you abuse me.' 'I know, I appreciate that you're angry, but it's abuse, and I won't let you abuse me...' It is hard to imagine how powerful this can be until you experience it, but those who are on the receiving end of 'broken record', even in role-play, will often comment on how determined the other person comes across.

And finally, there is the simple technique of *ignoring* a hurtful remark. None of us likes to be ignored, so your very silence may leave the abuser uncomfortable - and possibly more aware of the unfairness of their remark.

I'm not a machine!

These, then, are some ways of dealing with criticism and abuse that help you keep your dignity and self-respect, but the main skills are the two we have already met - levelling, (i.e. speaking personally, using 'I') and asking questions. If the abuse continues, you may need to repeat one of your 'I-messages', using the 'broken record' technique.

Now, you are not a machine - you may feel angry and frustrated by a put-down. Your self-esteem may take a battering. Don't be too discouraged if you lose your temper and say things you wish you hadn't said. We're all human, and it takes time to develop new habits. But it's good to find ways of coping with those angry feelings. Maybe you need to take some time and space to recover after a put-down. Focus onto something

Or go somewhere you can scream

completely different. Go for a walk, or take some strenuous exercise. Talk with a friend. Or thump a pillow in the bedroom and have a good cry. Or go somewhere you can scream. If you don't release your anger, it is liable to come out later in other ways - ill-health, depression, overeating, or an uncontrolled explosion that you may regret.

You are not a machine..

TABLE 3: DEALING WITH ABUSE AND CRITICISM

Below are some ways of dealing with abuse and criticism - but remember only to tackle small things for a start. You may be so powerless before an abusive teacher, for example, that it may be best to ignore that situation and concentrate on a situation where you <u>can</u> be assertive.

STAGE 1: IF CRITICISM *MAY* BE TRUE..

1. FIND OUT MORE - ASK QUESTIONS
`What makes you say that?.. Is that fair?..'

2. SAY YOU NEED TIME
`I want to think over what you've said..'

3. RECOGNISE WHAT'S TRUE IN IT
`Okay, I see your point. I just wasn't aware of this.'

4. AND TALK OUT CHANGES
`I wonder what would help?... What can we do so this doesn't happen again?'

STAGE 2: IF THE CRITICISM IS *NOT* TRUE

DENY IT CLEARLY AND DIRECTLY
`I've thought about what you said and I think you're being unfair to me - I've been doing my best.'

STAGE 3: IF YOU ARE NOT BEING RESPECTED..

When you are being abused or disrespected, you may be tempted to argue or go on the defensive. Instead, feel free to use any of the following approaches, or a mixture of them, depending on which you judge to be best in the circumstances, though at times it may be better simply to ignore the remark - or even to keep things light and humorous. Remember that you won't <u>win</u> with these methods - you will merely keep your dignity and make your abuser think.

ASK QUESTIONS	SPEAK PERSONALLY	BROKEN RECORD	USE 'FOGGING'
Excuse me? Why do you say that? Is it fair? How do you think I feel now?.. I see.	I feel hurt by that remark./ I don't like being labelled./ I'm doing my best./ No, I'm not an idiot.	I don't find that funny... Yes, I can understand why you said it, but I don't find it funny...	Mm.. Perhaps../ You could be right./ I'll have to think about it/ You're a laugh!

GETTING IN TOUCH

Here are some ways in which people feel put down.
1. Sarcasm - 'Oh, you're really thoughtful, I must say.'
2. Being interrupted - or ignored - when you're talking.
3. Being told to shut up.
4. Being treated without respect because you are a 'minor'.
5. Being patronised. 'Ah, you wouldn't know about this, dear.'
6. People making unfair assumptions (that young adults are all irresponsible, that a bad report means you're not working).
7. Remarks/ jokes that label women, men, gays, people of a particular race or job, people who are disabled...
8. Being scolded, nagged, bossed, shouted at.
9. Being treated as a sex object rather than as a person.
10. Hurtful jokes about your appearance, clothes, hair, glasses..
11. Being sneered at: 'You're always right!/ You know it all!'
12. Hurtful or crude words to describe you - stupid, fool, creep, dick-head, nuisance, wanker.

Who puts you down most? (Adults can be quite hurtful in the way they scold and boss young people, but young people - including brothers and sisters - can also be extremely hurtful to each other.) Can you remember one or two <u>specific</u> instances when you experienced someone treating you without respect? How did you feel? Form pairs, and take a few minutes to share your answers.

CASE STUDIES

Form groups of three, and take about five minutes as a group to decide how you might deal with the following put-downs in ways that are neither aggressive nor passive. Would you prefer to ask questions, or speak personally, or use 'fogging', or joke, or be silent, or use 'broken record'? What might you say in each case?:

Teacher or someone at work
You clumsy idiot!
I'll do it myself. You're making a mess!
You're not even trying!

Friend
You know everything, don't you!
Aw, shut up!
You wouldn't understand!

Parent:
Do what you're told! (*aggressively*)
Mind your own business!
That's not the way to do it!

Brother/sister
You're always showing off!
Where did you buy the jacket - a jumble sale?
You're a fat slob!

SKILL PRACTICE

First, take a few minutes to practise saying some of the phrases from Table 3, Stage 3. Say them assertively, looking directly and calmly at another person. Get some feedback on how you are coming across.

Next, an exercise to help you deal with abusive remarks in real life. One person says an abusive remark from the Case Studies above, and another deals with it. Each time, it helps to talk first about the approach you'll take, then deal with it in any of the ways suggested for dealing with abuse. After each situation, you can say how you felt, and get some feedback from the 'observer' on your tone of voice and body language. Change roles for each situation. Feel free to role-play a complete situation instead of just the opening lines, if you wish - for example using 'broken record'.

PLANNING FOR NEXT WEEK

Please read chapter four for next week - it is a great help to have the chapter read before each session.

Remind yourself of who it is that abuses you. Over the next week, you might tackle one or two fairly simple situations where you meet with abuse or criticism.

It is also suggested that you take some time each evening to relax your body and mind and become *aware* of how you have been assertive that day. Ask yourself, 'When today did I shrink from being honest? When did I choose to speak up, or to communicate more openly, or refuse to take abuse?.. Then, foresee how you will act in one situation you will be meeting the following day. Notice how you normally act, and then see yourself acting assertively - keeping your self-control but staying friendly. You may have to do this for a number of days before you see the difference in how you behave.

1. When will you take time each day to become aware and to foresee your behaviour?
2. Who criticises you? What will you do about it?...
Feel free to talk this out with the person beside you.

Plans... _____

_____

CHAPTER FOUR: WHEN YOU'RE ANNOYED OR ANGRY

In the last chapter we looked at how to deal with those who criticise or abuse you. Now we look at the other side of the coin - what to do when *you* are the one who is angry or annoyed and *you* feel the need to criticise or correct. It is an important topic, because you are going to go on meeting annoying situations all during your life, and how you handle them will affect the kind of friendships you have, the kind of marriage and family relationships you have, and the kind of person you become.

So how do you deal with annoying behaviour? With the passive, fearful approach, you try to avoid tension, so you do nothing about it, and 'hope' it will stop. That's not assertive because it doesn't respect yourself. It also means the other person doesn't have to look at their inconsiderate or disrespectful behaviour - they may not even become *aware* of it

With the passive approach, you try to avoid tension

The aggressive approach is to find fault and criticise. Almost without thinking, we get angry, or shout, or bully. We may feel better after that, but at what cost? People who are criticised a lot lose confidence in themselves and often perform more poorly. Marriages, families, and other relationships even split up as a result of so much criticism. Aggression often does more damage than the behaviour we want to correct. At the end of the last chapter we saw that there are other ways of releasing anger and frustration and rage without causing havoc.

'I need you to go easy.'

Neither of these approaches, then, is helpful - neither trying to bury our feelings alive nor taking them out on others. So how can we correct people in a way that avoids these extremes, and that is constructive and helpful and assertive? Let's look at an example.

Stewart has decided to talk with his mother about something that has been bothering him for some time. He says:

'Mum, I need to talk with you. When can we talk?'

'No time like the present,' she said, 'What is it?'

'No,' Stewart replied, 'I need time with you. Maybe about ten minutes. And we need to be sitting down so that you can listen to me properly.'

'Ten minutes?' his mother said, puzzled, 'What's this all about?'

'I don't really want to go into it until we can talk right, but I need to talk.'

'Okay,' his mother said, quite curious by now, 'We'll talk as soon as I have this finished.'

Half an hour later, they were sitting down together, and Stewart's mother asked him what he wanted to talk about.

'Mum,' he said, 'I don't think you realise it, but, as soon as you came in this evening, you started scolding everyone - about leaving the door open, and who left the knife on the table, and about me not changing out of my school uniform. It's depressing. I hate the evenings now - it's been happening a lot over the past few months. Besides, I'm seventeen, and it only gets my back up when you keep telling me what to do. I hate it. It makes me angry and it discourages me.'

Stewart's mother looked taken aback, even a bit defensive. She made as if to talk, but Stewart interrupted her.

'Let me finish, mum. I need you to hear me out; then **you** can talk. I just want to say that I know you've a tough day at work and it must be discouraging to come in and find that everything isn't the way you'd like it, so I can understand you being cross, but I need you to go easy on us. That's all.'

Choosing the right time

We'll stop here (though they still had some talking to do), and we'll look at what was

Aggression often does more damage than the behaviour we want to correct.

happening. This wasn't something petty, where Stewart had acted on the spur of the moment. It had been bothering him for some time, but he had waited for the right moment and had arranged a time with his mother. Nor was it a casual chat; he had asked for listening time, and that meant that his mother was in quite a different frame of mind when they eventually sat down together. He had a much better chance of being heard.

Very often, people just wade in and criticise anything that seems to be wrong. They don't wait for a suitable moment. This kind of spur-of-the-moment correction is as useless as waving at flies in annoyance. The flies won't go away. The annoyance will continue. Choosing the right moment, and checking out that it is a suitable time, is usually far more effective.

Giving an example

Secondly, Stewart was specific. He talked facts. Instead of talking in general terms ('You're always nagging!') he gave concrete, specific examples of the scolding - about leaving the door open, leaving the knife on the table, and not changing out of school uniform. You notice here that **he was critical of her *behaviour* and not of her*self*, not the *person*. It is never okay to attack a person's character, to call names or show disrespect.**

It was important, too, that Stewart limited himself to dealing with just one thing - his mother's scolding. This was not an opportunity for griping about old sores or other annoyances. It is recommended that you deal with only one problem or issue at a time. But what you say does need to be *specific*. People are much more likely to argue with you if you only talk in general. It is vital to have *examples*. If you are not sure of the facts, it may be better to postpone dealing with an annoying behaviour until you do have them.

A bald statement of the facts is not enough on its own, however - which brings us to the third guideline for dealing with an annoying behaviour.

Speaking personally

The third thing you will notice about what Stewart said is that he spoke personally. He told his mother how he *felt* about her behaviour ('angry', 'it discourages me', 'I hate it', 'it's depressing') and what his *needs* were in the situation ('I need you to go easy on us'). People are usually far more open to a criticism when you use 'I-statements' (about yourself) rather than accuse them with 'you-statements' - when you say, 'I feel nervous' rather than, 'You make me nervous'; 'I need you to go easy on me' rather than, 'You better go easy on me!'; 'It's important to me...' rather than, 'It's important for you...'

Speaking personally lets the other person know what you need and expect, and it also lets them know the effect of their behaviour on you. You're not saying that they *caused* your annoyance. You're not blaming. (After all, your feelings are your own; someone else in the exact same situation might feel quite differently.) You're merely saying that this is how you are. That may take courage, for they may not like what they hear, but it can be well worth the risk.

Some useful feeling words for giving constructive criticism are: annoyed, angry, upset, quite shocked, hurt, taken aback, taken for granted, disappointed, surprised, discouraged, lonely, sad, confused, disheartened, anxious, a bit frightened, scared, distant from you, tired, depressed, weary, disrespected..

End with something encouraging

Possibly the most interesting thing about what Stewart said was that he ended on a *positive* note. He showed understanding for his mother's situation. And that is the fourth and final guideline for dealing with annoying behaviour. After all, we have just seen that the goal is to criticise the behaviour and

'I need you to go easy'

not the person. When you give constructive criticism, it is good to end by saying something encouraging - for example, you could mention something positive that you have noticed about the person, or you could show some understanding for their situation. It is best if what you say is specific and brief - but always sincere.

Some people believe in saying something encouraging *before* making a criticism - the person being corrected may be less defensive as a result. But it seems to be even *more* helpful and effective to *end* constructive criticism by saying something encouraging. In this way, the last thing heard is positive. The person becomes aware of your goodwill. And that will often help them to hear what you are saying and may prevent them from going on the defensive.

There is no guarantee that this kind of constructive criticism will produce a change in behaviour. But it must have been sobering for Stewart's mother to hear what she heard. It will surely start them talking. They may need to do some negotiation (in another chapter we'll be looking at *how* to negotiate and talk something like this through). You can imagine, though, what a difference this approach might make in some homes, and what might happen as a result. Not enough parents hear this kind of thing.

'I thought I was special to you..'

Let's look at another example, this time between friends. Paul is angry about something he has heard. He needed to speak with his girlfriend, but he has thought about what he wants to say to her, and has waited for the right opportunity.

'Moya, I want to talk with you.'

'Talk away.'

'Not in front of the others. I need to talk with you on your own.'

They separated from the group and went off walking together. Paul didn't begin until they were well away from the others.

'I've discovered,' he said, 'That you were out with Ian yesterday.'

'I met him,' Moya said, 'I wasn't out with him.'

This was where it was essential to have facts. Otherwise, he could go no further.

'You were. Elaine saw you going into the park with him at eight o'clock.'

'Well, what if I was? You don't own me!'

Paul ignored the argumentative tone. He continued with an 'I-message'.

'I couldn't believe it when I heard you'd been out with him. It was like a slap on the face. My friends are probably all laughing behind my back now. I feel humiliated.'

'Don't take it like that. It was no big deal.'

'To me it was. I felt sick about it. I like you, and I thought you liked me.'

'I didn't think you'd take it like this... Anyway, I won't be going out with him again.'

In this case, Moya had been defensive to begin with, and she interrupted Paul a few times. But can you see how Paul was able to stick to the four basic steps and get through to her? - especially with his final (positive) statement.

Being flexible

That is not to say you should use this approach every time you meet with annoying behaviour. It is not for petty, on-the-spot annoyances. Besides, sometimes you can make your point quite effectively when you keep things light, use banter, or even say something outrageous - provided you know it will be taken in a spirit of fun. Moreover, it may not be appropriate in *your* home. You know best what is possible in your own situation.

'I've discovered you were out with Ian..'

Nor will it always work out as smoothly as in the example above. Constructive criticism like this is not something that comes naturally to us - especially ending on a positive note. It takes time, and some practice, before it begins to feel natural. As you practise, though, you can be quite flexible - you don't necessarily have to follow these four steps rigidly. You may need to begin by asking questions, for example. The other person may feel the need to give an explanation too - or they may be defensive and closed. But at least you will have a better chance of getting through to them this way. Maybe you'll see that more clearly in one further example.

`Were you reading my letters?'

Liz had arranged to talk with her father because she suspected that he had been reading her personal letters. Because she wasn't absolutely sure, she began wisely with a question rather than with an accusation. Looking him directly in the eye, she said:

'When you went into the bedroom this evening to read the paper, my drawer was closed, and I had letters in the drawer under a pile of things. I've just found the drawer slightly open, with the letters inside on *top* of my things. Were you reading them, Dad?'

'Maybe I was,' her father replied, defensively. 'I'm your father, and I need to know what's going on. If you don't tell me, I have to find out for myself.'

Liz did not take the bait. She resisted being drawn into an argument about whether or not he had a right to do what he had done. That's where this kind of confrontation often falls down. An 'I-message' is usually much more helpful - saying what she felt and what she needed.

'I'm your father, and I need to know what's going on.

'Dad,' she said, 'I'm shocked at what you've done. I have a right to keep some things private, and I need you to respect that.'

That was a powerful statement, and her father must have felt vulnerable, because he came back angrily.

'Now, look here,' he said, 'Don't you go talking to me about your rights! I have my rights too. I've a right to know what's going on!'

Liz decided to repeat her 'I-message' rather than argue, but she wanted her father to know that she had heard him.

'You have lots of rights,' she said, 'But reading my letters isn't one of them. I have a right to keep some things private, and I need you to respect that.'

'Nonsense! I have a duty as your father to check up on you!'

Liz felt as if she was getting nowhere - and we have seen that there's no guarantee that you'll win when you act assertively. She knew she couldn't force her father to change. But she still had a card to play - saying something that was both sincere and encouraging.

'Dad,' she said, 'You have a right to keep your things private too, and I would never read anything personal belonging to you. One of the things that I've always liked about you was that you *did* respect me and never opened my letters or anything like that. I need to know that you'll go on doing that and leave my personal stuff alone.'

That simple, positive statement got through to him.

'Well, when you put it like that,' he said, 'I suppose you have a point...'

It's not always as quick or as simple as this. You may have to negotiate about what changes need to be made so that both of you can have your needs met as far as possible. The person being corrected may also be quite uncooperative. If you are not being listened to or respected, you may need to use 'broken record', repeating again and again what it is specifically that you need or want, but avoiding aggression in your tone of voice, 'I hear what you're saying, but I need...'

Summing up

To sum up. In this chapter we have looked at four guidelines for giving corrections. The first is to choose an *appropriate time*. You can be much more effective when tempers have cooled down. The other person will then be better able to hear you.

Secondly, *be specific*. In talking with your father about his drinking, for example, it won't help to say, 'You're a drunk!' or, 'You've absolutely no control

'I was frightened when you shouted at Mum.'

over yourself!' but something direct and specific like, 'Twice during the holidays you'd had so much to drink that you staggered when you tried to walk and we had to help you up to the bedroom. You also shouted at us a lot.'

The third guideline is to *speak personally*. Not 'You'd better start taking control of your drinking!' which is a 'you-message' - although you may feel angry and want to say that. Better to say something like, 'I was frightened, especially when you shouted at Mum. Jane was crying and quite shocked. I felt awful.'

Finally, end on a *positive* note. Encouraging may be the last thing you feel like doing, but it may make all the difference. Be specific and sincere in what you say, 'I know you didn't realise what you were doing - that's why I'm talking with you now.' Or, 'I was so shocked because I've always admired you for the way you controlled your drinking.'

Needless to say, corrections like this will not come naturally off the tip of your tongue. They will take a bit of practice and will usually need to be prepared in advance. They may also sound stilted and awkward at first - so it does pay to think about what you'll say before you give constructive criticism.

When you do think out what you want to say, you may find you will make fewer criticisms, but that may be no harm. And what you do say may make you more effective in dealing with behaviour which upsets or annoys you, or which does not respect your rights or those of others. Constructive criticism will also serve to build up those around you instead of tearing them down.

TABLE 4: WHEN YOU NEED TO GIVE AN 'I-MESSAGE'

Here are four guidelines for dealing with behaviour that annoys you or makes you angry. The guidelines aim to help you give 'I-messages' in a constructive, respectful way. Which of these guidelines would you find most difficult?

1. CHOOSE A SUITABLE TIME Correction on the spot is often not appropriate.	'I'd like to talk with you. Is this a good time?'	'Are you free at the moment?.. Can I talk with you?..'
2. GIVE AN EXAMPLE Deal with only one problem at a time, and be specific.	'You took my sweater on Saturday night, and you didn't ask me if you could have it.'	'When I told you about Keith, I said it was just between you and me. I discovered yesterday you'd told Martin.'
SPEAK PERSONALLY Express your thoughts, feelings, needs, etc.	'I was annoyed you took it. I hate you taking me for granted or taking my things without asking.'	'I felt shocked and let down that you'd told him. When I tell you something personal, I need to know you won't talk about it.'
END ON POSITIVE NOTE. Show some understanding and appreciation for the person - at least that they meant well.	'I know it's not something you do a lot - you did ask me for a loan of my new socks last week. I need you to do that.'	'I'm telling you this because you're my friend - if you weren't my friend, I'd have gone off in a huff, and I wouldn't have bothered with you any more.'

GETTING IN TOUCH

What helps you to control your temper? Here are some ways that others have found helpful. Put a tick beside any of them that have ever helped you, and an X beside those you would like to try. Then you could chat to the person beside you about that.

Temporary methods

1. Leave the room, saying, 'I'm so angry I need to go away and come back when I'm calmer.'
2. Remind yourself, 'Losing my temper usually hurts others.'
3. Go and relax with deep breathing, or music.
4. Go for a walk.
5. Go and talk with a friend about it.
6. Think of something completely different - to change your feelings.
7. Tell yourself "I can handle this without getting angry'
8. Make plans about where to go from here.

Longer term: Ways of *releasing* the anger
Don't worry about feeling stupid or ridiculous - your body needs to get rid of negative feelings or you may become ill eventually. If possible, choose somewhere private to release anger.

9. Go to a bedroom, thump the mattress with a rolled-up newspaper, or with your fist (but don't hurt yourself), and say all you'd like to say - out of hearing, if possible.
10. Do something physical that requires strenuous effort (running, digging, swimming, cycling, cleaning..)
11. Have a good cry - tears can be a great release.
12. Twist a towel as if you were strangling it - and then bite into it.
13. If possible, go somewhere you can't be heard, and scream.
14. Write a letter to the person you're angry with, saying all you feel like saying; then tear up the letter.

CASE STUDIES:

Here are some situations which may make you feel annoyed or angry. As you read down the list, circle one or two feeling words in each case, then talk in pairs about how you'd feel, and tell each other about some similar situations in your own life.

1. You've discovered your mother has criticised you to others, e.g. saying she can't trust you to baby-sit. (Example of feelings: hurt, shocked, discouraged, angry, upset)
2. Your sister/ brother doesn't do the household chore that has been agreed on.
(Cheesed off, annoyed, taken for granted)
3. Your boss/ teacher/ parent wants to make decisions for you and is aggressive when you don't do things exactly as you're told. (Unimportant, resentful, small, disrespected, disheartened)
4. You've found out that someone you've been dating has also been dating one of your friends. (sick, disgusted, sad, shocked, humiliated, furious)
5. Your parents often come into your bedroom without knocking. Sometimes they open a drawer and read your personal things. (Disrespected, angry, taken aback, vulnerable, upset, unequal)
6. Your friend talks non-stop, and frequently interrupts you as soon as you start to speak. (Ignored, hurt, irritated, confused, frustrated, sad)
7. You share a room with your sister/brother, and have to listen constantly to their music - though your taste is different. (Annoyed, bored, frustrated, disrespected, ignored)
8. Your sister regularly borrows things from you and doesn't return them. (Frustrated, taken for granted, mad, fit to burst)
9. You have to listen to constant squabbling and fighting between two members of your family. (Sad, weary, depressed, frightened, want to escape, anxious)
10. One of your friends sponges on you a lot and seldom offers to contribute or pay for things. (Taken for granted, put off, disappointed, unequal, annoyed)

SKILL PRACTICE

Form groups of three and take turns in making up and then giving constructive I-messages for each of the above situations - or any other situation you need to deal with. Talk it out first, then practise it (check timing, be specific, say what you feel and need, e.g. for the first situation - 'Mum, can I talk with you?.. I've just discovered you told Mrs Bell you couldn't trust me to baby-sit. I felt shocked, and really hurt, that you'd talk about me behind my back like that. If you want to find fault, I need you to say things to my face'). After practising the skill, get feedback on body language.

The person being corrected doesn't make any reply - so that you can practise the skill more simply first.

PLANNING FOR NEXT WEEK

Please read chapter five for next week - it is a great help to have the chapter read before each session.

1. Which of the 'Case Studies' above reminded you of a situation you need to deal with? When would be a suitable time to speak with that person? What will you say?

2. Which of the suggested ways of controlling your temper would you like to try? When might that be? Feel free to share your answers with the person beside you.

Plans... _____

_____

CHAPTER FIVE: ENCOURAGEMENT AND ASSERTIVENESS

In chapter four, we saw how helpful it is to end a constructive criticism by saying something encouraging. In this chapter, we look more closely at this whole topic of encouraging, and we will see what an assertive thing it is to encourage people - and to accept a word of encouragement from others. We'll begin by looking at how we tend to react when someone says something encouraging or complimentary to us. Here's an example.

Unable to accept a compliment

Tina: 'You're looking well. I like your sweater.'

Denise: (embarrassed, and casting her eyes around in discomfort) 'Oh, I just put on the first thing I could find.'

Tina: 'But I really like it on you.'

Denise: 'This old thing? I've had it for years... But *you're* looking terrific...'

Denise finds it difficult to accept a compliment. She feels so uncomfortable with a compliment that she rushes to dismiss it. Then, when Tina attempts to reassure her, Denise continues to put herself down and desperately attempts to focus attention off herself on to her friend.

'My hair?... I'm not that happy with it myself.'

'You're looking well. I like your sweater.'

Does it sound familiar? The inability to accept compliments is very common. Many of us, when we receive a compliment, rush to shrug it off ('You must be joking!') or we put ourselves down ('I'm not much good at it really!') or we make a joke, or go into long explanations and excuses that show how uncomfortable we feel. Or, like Denise, we may be quick to turn the spotlight onto someone else. When someone says, 'Your hair's lovely,' we say something like, 'Look who's talking! - you're looking *really* well!' or, 'If you saw me ten minutes ago!' or, 'Do you think so? I'm not that happy with it myself.' Inside, we feel confused, perhaps hoping the compliment is true, but also thinking, 'My hair's probably a mess! I wonder why she said that? I wonder what she really thinks? Anyway, if I agree with her, she'll think I have ideas about myself!' Instead of accepting the compliment calmly, we may feel so uncomfortable that we don't even let it in.

We seldom appreciate ourselves

Have you ever noticed how easy it is to accuse yourself of being lazy or selfish even though you act lazily or selfishly only *some* of the time? - yet you won't accept that you're hard-working or generous if you only have *these* qualities some of the time. A virtue needs to be almost one hundred percent present before we accept it in ourselves, but a vice may only need to be ten per cent present to be accepted. It's a double standard. We live by two different standards a great deal of the time - so that we seldom appreciate ourselves, and we constantly live with a critical voice whispering in our ears. We become so convinced that this critical voice is right that we can't cope with a sincere compliment. Yet there is nothing either assertive or humble in cowering from the truth - we may never be properly assertive with others until we respect *ourselves*.

Not all reactions to compliments are so passive. Indeed, aggressive, put-down reactions are quite common among family members - including sarcasm and blunt contradiction ('What would you know!'/ 'Says who!'/ 'What are *you* looking for?' 'Don't be stupid - any fool can do that!' or 'Yeah. I've heard that before!') Don't be fooled by these aggressive reactions - they usually flow out of the same lack of appreciation for oneself. People don't usually mean to hurt you when they say things like this - they are just reacting desperately to hearing something positive about themselves.

'Don't be stupid - any fool can do that!'

Letting compliments in

How, then, do you become more assertive in accepting compliments? It is not difficult, although it may take some practice. You look directly at the person and thank them *briefly* and *simply* ('Thank you. I'm glad you told me that'), or you agree with the compliment, expressing a positive feeling, ('Thanks. I was pretty happy with it myself').

This approach has two advantages. First, it lets the compliment in. Instead of shrugging it off, we let it penetrate our defences. And that gradually seems to affect the way we see ourselves. It is lovely to see someone accept a compliment with a clear, direct look and an easy 'thank you' that indicates a healthy belief in themselves and a good self-image. The benefits of dropping barriers and letting in the good opinions of others can be considerable.

Secondly, we help the other person feel good about themselves when we accept their compliment as a gift. After all, it's frustrating to have a gift thrown back in your face - whereas it can be really encouraging when someone accepts your compliment and you know you've put a smile into their eyes. If, instead of saying, 'You're much better at it!' you say, 'Thank you. that's one of the nicest things anyone has said to me in a long time.' or, 'Thanks. It really helps me to hear that.' then the person giving the compliment is *also* encouraged.

'But they don't mean it!'

Now, that's all very well if a compliment is sincere. But what can you do if you suspect that people are saying flattering things to you that they don't mean?

Well, how do you know that a compliment is insincere? Isn't it possible that that's all part of the double standard we've just been talking about - we refuse to believe encouraging things about ourselves but we accept our own negative judgements to be correct. Anyway, even if someone is insincere in what they say, why should that make *you* less sincere - or ungracious? Why should you let someone else make you cringe or act aggressively? You can still be assertive and accept a compliment graciously. If you cannot honestly agree, 'Thanks, Mary, I was happy with the way it turned out,' you can at least agree in part, 'Thanks, Mary, I was pretty happy with it.'

'I'd be like a robot!'

Another objection is raised by those who react to saying a robot-like, automatic 'thank you' to every compliment. But you're not a robot. You have the freedom to thank people just as you have the freedom to develop any other good habit. What's so bad about having some polite, courteous habits? You don't *have* to say thanks, of course. With some friends, depending on the context, a perfect reaction may be to banter with them, even to tell them to go and see a psychiatrist! But do be careful - there is a difference between good-humoured banter and the type of joking that attempts to cover up the discomfort you feel at letting in the truth about yourself.

Giving compliments is also assertive

Another area that calls for assertiveness is in *giving* compliments and encouragement. The passive approach is to think of all kinds of reasons why you shouldn't tell others about the good impressions you have of them - 'They'd think it strange if I said something nice to them.' 'They might wonder what I was looking for.' 'I'll just do what everyone else does and drift along, so that nobody notices me or thinks me odd.'

Aggressive attitudes also prevent us from saying things that are encouraging. Criticising people, shouting at them, or putting them down can be so common in some families that it is sometimes seen as the *normal* way to treat each other. (Yet this destructive criticism is sometimes confused with assertiveness!)

Assertiveness is not just about standing up for your rights and sharing your negative feelings with others. It also includes telling people about what you see in them that impresses you. If it is assertive to express your thoughts and feelings openly with your family and friends, shouldn't that include your *positive* feelings and impressions as well? 'I like that colour on you.' 'Thanks for doing that - I really appreciated it.' 'I love you.' 'I'm happy with the way you handled that.'

How to give compliments that strike home

Expressing these positive feelings usually makes a compliment more effective and helps it to strike home, for a good compliment will often include feelings and be *personal*. Many sincere compliments are not effective simply because they are not personal. They use 'you' instead of 'I'. They say, 'You're great!' - instead of, 'I like the way you get along with people.' Or, 'You're a very good driver' - instead of, 'I feel relaxed when you're driving.' Expressing positive feelings is a powerful way to build up those we come into contact with.

Another thing that helps a compliment to strike home and build someone up is to give an example, to make what you say *specific*. You can say, 'You're wonderful' about anyone, but when you say, 'I was watching how you handled that situation, and I'm impressed - you looked directly at him and didn't lose your cool,' that will come across as much more encouraging because it is specific. When you say something general to your friend, like, 'You're super!' she may or may not find that helpful, but when you say, 'Thanks for finding the book for me. I'm so relieved to have it,' she will have a much clearer sense of being noticed and appreciated.

As with all assertive skills, something is missing from any compliment if you are looking at your shoes as you talk. Your body language needs to match what you're saying. To be assertive, it helps to look straight at the person you're giving a compliment to and to speak calmly, without an apologetic stammer or longwinded explanation.

But there's nothing to praise!

But what do you do if you can find nothing to encourage? What if a family member or a friend is extremely rude and disrespectful? Well, as we have seen, there are other assertive skills for dealing with

'Thanks for finding the book for me. I'm so relieved to have it,'

disrespect or put-downs. You're not expected to make yourself a doormat or to attempt to offer a compliment to someone who has just humiliated you. But when people are rude to you, it may also help to remember that they're usually feeling miserable inside. In a situation like that, maybe the most encouraging thing you could do is understand that they are in pain.

In some cases, however, we don't see the good in others because we're wearing the same dark glasses that prevent us from seeing the good in ourselves. Yet everyone has good qualities. At the end of any day, you can look back and think of a number of times when *you* made an effort or acted responsibly or kindly; the same is true for others. They are also making an effort. The good points are there if we look for them. Perhaps the secret is to stop looking for 'perfection', (which may only make us more aware of the flaws), and to practise looking out for *little* efforts. Regularly noticing something positive can go a long way towards building people up and improving the way they see themselves.

What an eighteen year old wrote

It's not just a matter of what you *say*, though. When it comes to building others up, actions usually speak louder than words. Think about that for a moment and ask yourself what your own experience is. When have *you* ever felt encouraged? What has

'I feel relaxed when you're driving.'

helped you to feel good about yourself? Here is what eighteen year old Alan wrote in answer to that question:

'I remember a girl I liked smiling at me as she passed me in the street. Not a "come-on" smile - just a friendly smile that seemed to say she liked me. I felt so great I could have jumped over a house...'

'I remember cups of tea my mother brought up to my bedroom when I was studying for an exam, and she'd put a special biscuit, or sometimes a chocolate bar, on the plate beside it. It was the thought behind it - I felt cared about...'

'I also remember the awful feeling of failing the exam and coming home to an empty house. My sister came in, and I said "I failed!" and she put her arms around me - a sister I used to fight about everything with! But when I most needed someone, she was there for me. And when I looked at her she had tears in her eyes. I'll never forget that. I wasn't so alone any more...

Do Alan's memories help you get in touch with a time when you felt encouraged? Did you notice that it was some *action*, something that someone *did* rather than what they said, that made the difference for him? That is the power each of us has to build up the people we meet. **We can put a smile into their eyes instead of fear. And we can do that with something as simple as a friendly nod, a smile, an unexpected gift, a touch on the arm as we pass, a thoughtful act, a hug, being willing to listen...**

What prevents us from encouraging?

What is it that prevents us, then, from loving, encouraging, or caring in these ways?.. For some of us, it may be the way we drift along, caught in the rut of the next exam, or the next wage packet, or the next promotion, and we don't take time out to think about what we really want. That is one of the reasons for this course - to help us stop in our tracks and ask ourselves what we do want in life.

For others of us, it may be *feelings* that prevent us from encouraging. If we feel loving, it can be fairly easy to show kindness and warmth, but how do we cope when we feel nothing? - or when we feel dislike or hatred? Some of us may be quite miserable, for example, when we no longer have feelings of love for a parent - when almost everything a parent does even irritates us and drives us up the wall. It may be assertive to encourage, but how can we be loving or encouraging then? Worse still, how will we cope when, one or two years into marriage, we realise we have 'fallen out of love'?

It can come as a great relief to those who have negative feelings like these when they realise that it's okay not to feel any love at times. It's perfectly normal. It shows you're human. And yet loving feelings will usually come back soon once we move out of ourselves and do something kind or thoughtful. It's not easy, but it is possible to *decide* to be thoughtful, or friendly, or even to think about something we *used* to like about the person. This is possible even when we have *no* positive feelings, even when we're *mad* with someone and feel we hate them. So my relationship with my parents is not at an end if I have no feelings of love. And my marriage will not be dead some day if I find I have 'fallen out of love'. Love isn't just a feeling.

Freeing ourselves to love

There may be another reason why we don't find it easy to love or encourage others - because many of us are so busy coping with our own pain, particularly the pain of not liking ourselves very much. Sometimes we look in the mirror and see only the things that are 'wrong' with us, the things we don't like about ourselves. It's hard to love others when we have a deep pain like that inside. Instead, we look for ways to 'cope'. We fill our minds and our senses with distractions. We crave for chocolate, or another cigarette, or we overeat, or we become television addicts, or we bury ourselves in books, or in work, or we look to drugs or drink or sex to help us forget the pain of who we are, even to help us not to *feel* the pain. In this way we may begin to lose control of our lives. We may believe that love is important, but loving or encouraging are much less possible when we do not love ourselves.

So what can you do? There are lots of suggestions in self-help books. They emphasise thinking positively. Looking in the mirror every morning, for example, and saying, 'I'm beautiful.' Or regularly repeating, 'I like myself.' You can try

'I don't have to be perfect. It's okay to be the way I am'

things like that and see what works for you. But some of these suggestions seem a bit superficial - like attempts to cover up the cracks on the surface. It's hard to beat honesty. Maybe it would be better to recognise that you're not very beautiful after all - but that you're not as messed up as you often feel. Maybe you could look in that mirror and say to yourself, 'I'm not perfect, and I'm never going to be perfect, and I don't *have* to be perfect. It's okay to be the way I am - warts and all.'

Those who lower their sights and settle for being less than perfect may still work at improving, but once they accept that it's okay to be imperfect, they find they have less to hide, they spend less energy trying to impress, they often feel happier in themselves - and they may begin to like themselves more. That can free them to love.

Summary

In this chapter we have seen that giving and receiving compliments is an area where we can fall down in being assertive. In order to accept a compliment graciously, it helps to *look directly* at the other person and *thank them*, perhaps expressing a positive feeling, 'Thanks for telling me that. I'm glad you told me.'

In giving encouragement, it also helps to look directly at the person and to speak *personally and specifically*. Doing something thoughtful, or showing a little kindness, may be even more helpful than words in building people up and helping them to feel better about themselves. That can be difficult. It's easier to wear a mask, to act tough, to be 'cool' - to try to hide the insecurity and pain that many of us suffer from. And yet, deciding to move out of ourselves, to be thoughtful, to stay friendly, or to look for the good points in those we live and mix with, will often bring back positive feelings and make it easier to love. The first step, we saw, may be to decide to lower our sights and accept our imperfect selves just as we are.

Deciding not to act on feelings is not just good for ourselves. Can you think of anyone you have ever met who believed in you, or liked you, or listened well to you, or helped you to feel okay? Can you remember how that person made you feel? The message of this chapter is that we have the same power to bring new life and encouragement to our families and friends.

It's easier to wear a mask, to be 'cool..'

TABLE 5: GIVING AND RECEIVING COMPLIMENTS

You are not expected to use all of the guidelines below in any given situation. Choose what you feel is appropriate, and use only words that are natural for you.

SOME WAYS OF RECEIVING COMPLIMENTS....

LOOK OPENLY AND DIRECTLY AT THE PERSON - not at the ground.

THANK THE PERSON - AND EXPRESS A POSITIVE FEELING 'Thanks, Sandra, I'm glad you liked it.'/ 'Thanks, Joe, I'm pleased you told me that.'/ 'Thanks, it really helps me to hear that.'/ 'Thanks, Alan, I was happy with the way it turned out.' (If you cannot honestly agree, then agree in part, 'Thanks. I was pretty happy with it.')

KEEP YOUR REPLY SHORT - a long reply, with explanations or excuses shows your lack of ease with the compliment and prevents you from letting it in.

....AND OF GIVING COMPLIMENTS

LOOK OPENLY AND DIRECTLY AT THE PERSON when you give a compliment, and speak simply, without apology or hesitation.

CATCH OTHERS DOING RIGHT - To do this, it helps to think positively about others, not looking for excellence - just for some effort, or a little improvement, or something that helped you or that you *liked*, 'That was a good help to me - thanks a lot.' 'Thanks for the dinner. It was lovely - especially the soup.' 'I like that jacket on you - really suits you.'

BE SPECIFIC AND BRIEF - Avoid general comments like, 'You're great/ you're very good.' Mention *specifically* the behaviour you liked, 'I was impressed at how you kept your cool. What's your secret?' 'I'm pleased you got the stain out of my sweater. Thanks a lot.'

USE 'I' 'I liked..' 'I was happy about... 'I feel relaxed and safe with you when you're driving.' 'I was impressed with the way you..' 'I'm delighted you did that.' 'Well done. I thought you handled him well - he can be difficult.' 'Thanks for listening - I feel much better.'

BE SINCERE - A genuine compliment is always truthful. Avoid flattery or exaggeration.

GETTING IN TOUCH

Here are some things people say when they receive a compliment. Do you ever make similar comments when you're complimented? Tick any that apply:

AGGRESSIVE (Macho reaction, often with our own families)

- **Contradict other's judgement.** 'Don't be stupid! Anybody can do that!'
- **Attack the other's motives.** 'What are you looking for!'
- **Sarcasm.** 'Oh. You've noticed me at last.'
- **Reject compliment dismissively.** 'How would you know!'
- **Boast.** 'Yeah. I'm the best!'

PASSIVE/ APOLOGETIC (Common reaction when with friends)

- **Don't let it in, shrug it off.** 'Did you think so? I wasn't that happy with it myself.'
- **Make a joke.** 'You want my autograph?'
- **Put self down.** 'Me?! If you'd seen me this morning!'
- **Turn spotlight off self by complimenting someone else.** 'Naw - you're much better at it than me.'
- **Go into long explanations**

CASE STUDIES

Form groups of three, and talk about what you see wrong with each of the compliments below - Using 'you' instead of 'I'?/ patronising?/ exaggerated?/ not specific?/ comparing to others?/ not personal?

'You're wonderful!'
'You're doing a grand job, dear.'/
'Ninety right! That's fantastic!'
'That's better than Peter! Terrific!'
'You're a great girl!'/

Next, what do you think is wrong with each of these things, said by people when they had <u>received</u> a compliment? (Check the 'Getting in Touch' section if necessary.)

'It's no big deal!'
'If you only knew the truth!'
'This coat? I got it cheap in a sale!'
'My hair? Don't be daft - look at the state of it!'

Can you remember one time when someone said something encouraging to you - or about you? How did you feel?

SKILL PRACTICE

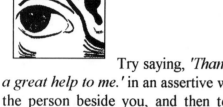

Try saying, *'Thanks, that was a great help to me.'* in an assertive way - first to the person beside you, and then to the wider group. Get feedback on whether or not you are coming across in a relaxed, assertive way.

Secondly, tick at least six of the following qualities you have - not all the time, but at least *some* of the time. Generosity, sense of fun, warmth, sincerity, thoughtfulness, good humour, sense of justice, honesty, reliability, friendliness, sense of responsibility, patience, gentleness, openness, being relaxed, a good listener..

Which of these do you most like about yourself?

PLANNING FOR NEXT WEEK

Please read chapter six for next week - it is a great help to have the chapter read before each session.

Choose from the suggestions below in planning for the week ahead. Feel free to have a chat with the person beside you in order to talk out what you will do.

1. Who do you tend to find fault with most? (This is usually someone in your own family.) Even if you find it too difficult to encourage that person, you might at <u>least</u> stop criticising them.

2. Over the next week, (indeed, for the rest of your life!), you might try giving compliments at least once each day. The more you practise, the more the habit will become second nature to you. Who can you encourage in the next 24 hours? What have you liked about them, and how can you make what you say personal?

3. Encouragement is not just a matter of what we <u>say</u>. Actions speak louder than words. Doing something thoughtful for someone in your family without being asked, even giving them an unexpected hug, or sitting down and listening to them, can be very encouraging. You have *great* power to help others feel better about themselves and put a smile into their eyes. Who will you be kind to at home, and what will you do?

Plans...

CHAPTER SIX: LISTENING AND ASSERTIVENESS

'Stop worrying!'

In chapter five, we looked at ways of giving and receiving encouragement. In this chapter, we now move on to look at what is perhaps the best possible way of encouraging people - listening to them and giving them a sense of being understood. We'll begin by looking at how we often fail to listen to each other.

Mother: 'Sandra's out very late. I wonder where she is?'

Kevin: 'Look, Mum, don't go on and on about her!'

Mother: 'What do you mean? I'm not going on and on. This is the first time I've mentioned Sandra.'

Kevin: 'Maybe it's the first time this *evening*, but you do go on about her!'

Mother: 'But she's never as late as this.'

Kevin: 'Look, she's okay! Will you give over!'

Mother: 'That's easy for you to say. I'm her mother, and I have to care about her!'

Kevin: 'And I'm her brother, and I know she can take care of herself. Now, will you stop worrying!'

On one level, this is a kind enough conversation, and you may think Kevin sounds pretty reasonable. He obviously wants the best for his mother, wants to reassure her, and to stop her worrying unnecessarily. But do you think his approach will help? Telling people to 'stop worrying' isn't usually effective. Even his attempt to reassure her that Sandra can look after herself will scarcely be helpful; 'reassuring' instead of listening does not give people what they deeply need - a chance to express how they are feeling, and a sense of being understood. Kevin is not doing that.

'Look, don't go on and on about her!'

How we fail to listen

There are many ways in which we don't listen. One 'passive' approach, for example, is to go through all the motions, nod your head and say, 'I know' and 'Uh-huh' and 'I'm with you' - but you're only pretending to listen; you may be thinking of what you're going to say next, or what question you'll ask when the speaker has stopped. Another passive approach is when you're so desperate to be liked that you agree with everything the speaker says, you tell them they were absolutely right to do what they did, you console them, you make suggestions, you offer advice. This is usually done with the best of intentions, but it is a poor substitute for really listening and trying to understand.

Then there are aggressive ways of not listening. With the aggressive approach you don't pretend to listen. You simply tune out family members and friends in a number of different ways. For example, you don't turn towards them when they are speaking, or you don't look at them, or you fold your arms. Another way to show with your body language that you're not listening may be the expression on your face - you frown, or you deliberately look bored or hostile. Or you act in a bullying manner, listening only to argue or contradict.

Other ways of not listening include interrupting, joking when the other person is being serious, or asking questions that distract - or that put the speaker on the defensive.

What all these forms of non-listening have in common is that they do not respect the speaker. A lack of respect is never assertive, for assertiveness is rooted in respect. In the situation above, where Kevin is talking with his mother, assertive, respectful listening might look something like this:

'I had no idea...'

Mother: 'Sandra's out very late. I wonder where she is?'

Kevin: 'Yeah... She is a bit late.'

Mother; 'She's never as late as this...'

Kevin: 'Mm...' (pause) 'You're worried?..'

Mother: 'Well, I do worry about her...'

Kevin: 'Yeah?...'

Mother: 'It's those boys she's got in with...'

Kevin: (pause) 'You're not happy about them...

Mother: 'No. Not really. They scare me. I know she has to live her own life, but I'd hate to see her getting hurt...'

Kevin: 'And you think she might..

Mother: 'Yes... Sometimes I can't sleep at night

51

'I had no idea it was so upsetting for you...'

just thinking about her. I can't stop myself worrying.'

Kevin: 'Mm... Sounds like.. it's a.. *huge* worry for you

Mother: 'Well, it is really..'

Kevin: 'That's hard, mum. I had no idea it was so upsetting for you...'

Mother: 'Oh, I suppose I'm just an old worrier!...'

Can you imagine how Kevin's mother will begin to feel if she is listened to regularly like that? No one is telling her to shape up, or to change her feelings, or that the way she feels is not okay. She is being given the freedom to talk and is being encouraged to say more ('Mm...' 'Yeah?..' 'And you think...') And she has experienced some real understanding ('Sounds like it's a *huge* worry...' 'That's hard.' 'I had no idea...') You can see how this kind of listening could create a totally different atmosphere of respect and understanding in a family or among friends.

What is it that makes this difference to the quality of our listening? Are there some rules for good listening that can be practised and learnt?

Tips on listening

We have to be careful here not to over-simplify or to reduce listening to a mere technique, for we have just seen that it is quite possible to go through all the motions of listening, to say little, to look interested, to nod your head occasionally and say, 'mm', and 'yes' and 'uh-huh'. These are good things. Making a comment now and again in a gentle, caring tone is usually a *sign* of good listening. But **such things can never be substitutes for genuinely** *caring* **and wanting to** *understand***, nor for paying good attention to what someone is saying.**

That said, here are some things good listeners often do: You will notice that they listen with their *eyes*. You can *see* interest and caring in their eyes - they don't stare, but it's obvious from the way they look at you that they are paying attention (how do *you* feel when you are talking with someone who is looking at the floor, or at a wall, or at their watch, or out the window!) Good listeners will usually listen with their whole body. They turn towards you, even *lean* towards you, and you will notice that, as they become more interested in what you are saying, they may unfold their arms or uncross their legs.

There are other things you may notice. Good listeners are normally slow to interrupt, to ask questions, or joke, or advise, or even console. There is a time for consoling, but well-meaning people are sometimes too quick to jump in to console instead of holding back and allowing the speaker to say more. As your listening improves, you will probably have to allow yourself to become comfortable with silence, for there are often periods of silence during good listening, and some people find it difficult not to rush in and fill them up. After a silence, a listener will often repeat some of the speaker's words, and that seems to encourage the speaker to say a little more. A helpful listening skill, too, is occasionally to sum up in your own words what has been said and check out that you have understood.

Do you have to dump your things here!

This idea of summing up what the speaker has said brings us to a special kind of listening that people find particularly helpful. It's often called 'active' or 'reflective' listening because you don't just listen passively in silence; you make an active effort to 'reflect' back to the speaker what you hear. The important thing is to listen for how the other person is *feeling*, and to sum up or reflect that. When you

You will notice that they listen with their eyes.

Do you have to dump your things on my bed!

check out if you are correct, that can give the speaker a sense of being listened to and understood. Maybe it will help to give an example. Here are a brother and sister talking together:

Chris: (very angrily) Look, do you have to dump your things on my bed!

Sonya: (picking them up) Sorry about that... (pause) How are things anyway?

Chris: Lousy! Things are always lousy!

Sonya: Mm... Had a tough day?..

Chris: Yeah!... As if you cared!

Sonya: (ignoring the put down) Maths again, is it?

Chris: Naw, it's the whole school crap... I wish I could leave the crappy place this summer. It stinks!

Sonya: You sound very fed up with it...

Chris: Yeah. I'm really pissed off with the whole crappy place, and those crappy teachers, and those crappy stupid idiots in my class!

Sonya: The whole lot of them..

Chris: Yeah, the whole crappy lot of them... Especially Julian.

Sonya: You don't like him..

Chris: He's a two-faced bugger.

Sonya: You sound very annoyed with him..

Chris: Annoyed? I'm pissed off with him. I told him I fancied Rachael and what did he do! - f****** dated her himself.

Sonya: (genuinely shocked and distressed for her brother) Oh!.. That was really hurtful!

Chris: (softening) I just can't believe that he could do something like that.

Sonya: You don't expect a *friend* to act like that..

Chris: Some friend... Anyway, I'd better get down to work here. Thanks. It's good to talk with someone.

It's difficult to listen like that, isn't it! It takes almost a superhuman effort not to react to someone in such a negative mood. On one level, Chris was screaming for someone to listen to him, and at the same time, he was putting up all kinds of barriers. It was like a coded cry for help. Someone had to break the code before he could admit what it was that was really upsetting him. Aren't we often like that when we have strong feelings? It's almost as if we feel too vulnerable, so it's easier to be bitter and angry.

Sonya had sensed there was more to her brother's bad humour. Yet she didn't move in on him too quickly, or ask him what was wrong - he might only have reacted and insisted he was fed up with having things dumped on his bed. She made a number of attempts before he began to open up. He also said a lot of silly things that you might have been tempted to argue with if someone said them to you ('things are always lousy..' 'school stinks...' 'there are idiots in my class...' 'he's a bugger..') But then we do tend to say things like that when we're upset.

Listening for feelings

And yet, far from arguing with him, Sonya allowed him to say more. She did this especially by listening beyond his words to how he seemed to be *feeling*, and she kept checking out if the feeling she was hearing was correct ('fed up...' 'you don't like...' 'you're annoyed..' 'that's hurtful..') Gently reflecting back in your own words what you hear is central to active listening.

How is this 'reflecting' done? It is usually best not to ask questions in a case like this, for questions can sometimes be a bit threatening and may close people up. You might start very simply by looking carefully as you listen, watching even for feelings that are not mentioned at all, and then you check out with, 'You feel... because... ('You feel depressed because you've so much work to do for the exams..'; 'You're feeling angry because she walked past you and didn't speak with you..') At first, this may seem

'Anyway... it's good to talk to someone.'

to be a strange or unnatural thing to do - though people who are feeling angry or upset will usually be so glad to express their feelings that they probably won't notice anything strange. As you become more confident, you'll find lots of ways of reflecting back what you hear in a more natural way ('Yeah, it's depressing, isn't it, when you've so much work to do...' 'Sounds like you're feeling...' 'You must feel...' 'You seem very...' 'You sound...)

Listening can work wonders

This kind of listening should not be overdone. It need only be used when someone seems to have strong feelings. But wouldn't it be nice to have someone in your family who could be as patient and caring as Sonya in the example above? With practice you could be that person yourself.

You can imagine, as well, how useful it would be to be able to listen like this to a marriage partner or other friend in the future. Many marriage counsellors recommend couples to do an exercise like this a few times a week, taking turns to talk about their day for a few minutes, then summing up what they heard each other say and feel. Couples often surprise each other when they do this - these two people who are living in the same house and who assume they know each other. Listening to each other like this prevents them from taking each other for granted, and it's a good way to build their relationship. You might try it now and again with a friend, for it's a great way to get closer to someone and build *any* friendship.

Even when active listening is not appropriate, there is *always* a place for ordinary good listening - deciding to pay attention to what those we meet are saying and feeling. It's an assertive, respectful thing to do, and some people think that it's the greatest thing we can ever do for another person. Instead of offering 'solutions' or advice, we can be more helpful to people with a problem when we just give them a sense of being listened to. They can then solve their *own* problems. Listening is often the only solution that's needed.

But let's come back to this idea that good listening is a powerful way to develop closeness between people and to allow friendships to grow. All too often, we stay on the surface with our friends and family, we react as we have always reacted, or we joke and make fun - which is good, too, but it means that we can miss out on a deeper experience. Here is an example.

I'm not in the mood

Darren and Lorraine had been going out together

'I'm not in the mood,' she said.

for a few months. Darren really liked her because she looked so pretty and so sexy. One evening, as they came to the alley-way where they usually kissed and cuddled, Lorraine said she didn't want to stop.

'I'm not in the mood,' she said.

'What do you mean you're not in the mood?' Darren asked. 'I often do things when I'm not in the mood! Besides, *I'm* in the mood. Come on, Lorrie.'

'No, Darren. Don't push me. I'm really not in the mood.'

Darren felt annoyed, even a bit hurt. But he liked Lorraine. She was different. And that helped him to make the decision not to push things but to listen instead. They walked on.

'Want to talk about it?' he asked.

There was a longish silence.

'Things aren't great at home,' she said

Another silence. Darren said nothing, just put his hand into hers. She continued.

'There's a lot of fighting between my Mum and Dad. It gets to me. It's depressing even to go into the house..'

Her voice was breaking as she spoke. Tears

usually turned Darren off, but on this occasion he felt as if he was actually feeling along with her. He slipped his arm around her waist. It seemed the natural thing to do.

'It's very upsetting for you...' he said.

She told him about a big row that had flared up that evening, how her parents had shouted and screamed and thrown things at each other and how she and her younger sister had felt terrified in the midst of it all.

When she had finished talking, there was a pause. Then Darren spoke:

'That's terrible. It must have been awful for you...'

Lorraine had never experienced this side of Darren before. A softer, gentler side, that was listening and compassionate. She felt freer to talk, and she opened up and talked with him as she never had before. For the first time she began to see him as a friend, someone she could trust and talk things over with - rather than just a 'boyfriend'.

Discovering the person

If it was a new experience for Lorraine, it was a real revelation to Darren. He really didn't know what had possessed him to listen instead of reacting to her 'bad mood'. But he was bowled over by her trust. It was hard to describe how he felt, but he had a sense of privilege to know Lorraine like this, even in her misery. She had trusted him. There was a new bond between them, and a new kind of relationship that was no longer just founded on sexual attraction.

What really happened here was that Darren and Lorraine had met as *persons*. Their relationship had been quite superficial until now. Perhaps this was the crucial 'make or break' time, and Darren's listening had opened up the possibility of a deeper friendship. They were getting to know and appreciate each other as whole persons, as friends, rather than merely as sex objects. Experts on relationships tell us that this is an important stage in the development of male-female relationships.

Because of the new and powerful sexual urges that adolescents and young adults experience, it is natural for them to be fascinated by sexual *parts* - each other's skin, breasts, hair, lips, legs, clothes, bottoms.. Part of growing in maturity means moving from that fascination with each other as sexual *objects* (and part-objects) to an awareness and appreciation of each other as whole persons. That is what we have just seen beginning to happen between Lorraine and Darren. Real intimacy is developing. And listening seems to be the key to it.

Many young couples choose to marry or live together today because of sexual attraction. This physical attraction is something wonderful, and they naturally want it to last. The message of this chapter is that it *can* last. It is the experience of couples who are married for many years that sex can become a deeper, more enjoyable and more fulfilling experience as communication and intimacy improve. Good communication, especially good listening, is a great foundation on which to build a long term relationship.

Listening is a decision

There is something else in the story of Darren and Lorraine that is worth highlighting. You notice that Darren *decided* to listen. Listening did not just 'happen'. It took a decision to put aside his own worries and concerns, even his strong personal feelings of anger and sexual attraction, and to zone in on Lorraine as a person. That meant not acting on

seeing him as a friend, someone she could trust..

his feelings. Good listening can call for a good deal of self-control and assertiveness.

Be warned, though. As you become a better listener, more people will tend to confide in you. You will need to resist the pressure to give them answers. And you may need to protect yourself against the person who *always* has a problem - and the one who takes two hours to tell a story, often the same story each time. The decision to listen does not mean deciding to become a doormat.

Summary

In this chapter we looked at how we often fail to listen, and how we can improve our listening. We saw that good listening includes looking at the speaker, watching out for feelings, and checking out that you understand as you reflect back in your own words what you hear. But it is not a question of techniques. Listening is a decision - a decision to *care* about another person, to put aside everything else, to pay attention, and discover the *person* rather than a 'problem' to be solved. It is an assertive life skill that can give us great power to free up those around us, and to build better relationships and deeper friendships. It would also seem to be a key way of growing in maturity.

TABLE 6: HOW WE LISTEN

Good listening is a vital assertive skill, for it is an important way of respecting others. Below are some examples of how we fail to respect people by not listening to them - and of how we might listen and encourage them to say more. The listening comments below may not be your words - the words will vary with different people and different situations. But what effect do you think comments like these might have on you?

REMARK	POOR LISTENING **We impose our ideas or close off the conversation instead of allowing other person to open up.**	GOOD LISTENING **We encourage others to say more by staying neutral or reflecting back a little of what we hear.**
Friend: The Maths teacher hates me!	*She hates everybody - she's a creep/* **or** *Don't be silly - it's your imagination!*	*That's hard. Maths is tough enough without feeling she doesn't like you.*
Father: I don't think he's good company for you	*Mind your own business!* **or** *It's my life - I'll decide who's good company for me!*	*You're not too happy about me getting friendly with him...*
Your sister: I really like Martin.	*He's a jerk! Nobody in their right mind.../* **or** *Watch him! I don't trust him.*	*Do you?... Tell me about him..*
Friend: Oh, I got on great on Saturday...	*Me too - wait till you hear what happened../* **or** *Oh, where are you going next Saturday?..*	*Great! What did you do?..*
Mother: It's weeks since we got a letter from granny.	*Is that all you have to worry about!/* **or** *She's okay. She can take care of herself!*	*You're worried because you haven't heard from her...* *Say more, Mum...*
Young Brother: I earned two pounds!	*That's nothing. I earn that in half an hour!* **or** *Oh, give over! You're always going on about money!*	*Two pounds! What are you going to buy?..*

GETTING IN TOUCH

Here is a list of ten things which we sometimes do when we are not listening. Tick any of them which you tend to do quite often.

Now tick any of the ten ways in which you tend to listen reasonably well. Don't be too hard on yourself - you can tick things you sometimes do. You don't have to be perfect before you give yourself a tick. When you have finished, have a chat with the person beside you about how you ticked the two lists.

SIGNS OF POOR LISTENING

1. Not looking at the person who is speaking.
2. Folding your arms - or turning away from the speaker.
3. Frowning, looking bored, or hostile, while person is speaking.
4. Interrupting.
5. Thinking of what you'll say or ask next.
6. Joking when the other person is being serious.
7. Only listening in order to argue or contradict.
8. Asking questions that distract or put person on the defensive.
9. Offering advice or suggestions instead of listening.
10. Consoling or reassuring instead of trying to understand.

SIGNS OF GOOD LISTENING

1. Paying attention and looking at the person.
2. Turning your body, even leaning towards speaker.
3. Showing care and interest, especially with eyes.
4. Opening your arms and uncrossing your legs.
5. Slow to interrupt, to ask questions, joke, advise or console.
6. Remaining silent, with occasional nod or 'mm', 'yes', 'uh-huh.'
7. Making comment at times in a gentle, caring tone.
8. Occasionally summing up or checking you understand.
9. Repeating some of speaker's words after a silence.
10. Most important of all, really *caring* and wanting to understand

CASE STUDIES

The feelings behind the following remarks will depend on how they are said. But what do you think some of the feelings might be:

1. Brother: 'Shut up, would you! I told you I was feeling okay!'
2. Mother: 'I said you had to be home at eleven! What kept you?'
3. Jackie:(to friend of opposite sex) 'I'd like to go out with you.. What do you think?..'

Now, what feelings might be behind each of the remarks in the first column of Table 6?

PLANNING FOR NEXT WEEK

Please read chapter seven for next week - it is a great help to have the chapter read before each session.

Over the next week, it is suggested that you practise being assertive at least once each day, and that you give a number of your friends and family members a good experience of being listened to. The more interest you show, the more they will feel respected and the more they will tend to open up to you. You could make your plans from some of the ideas below.

1. Who do I have difficulty in listening to? (This is usually someone in your own family!) What would help?

2. Who will I listen to in the next 24 hours or so? What could I show an interest in? How will I get them talking?

Plans... _____

_____

CHAPTER SEVEN: PROBLEMS!

Mother: Ian, your room is an absolute mess! It's a disgrace! Really *disgusting*!

Ian: My room is my room! *You* can keep your room whatever way you like, but keep your nose out of mine - that's my business!

Mother: This *is* my business. What would anyone think if they saw the state of it at this moment! I don't know how your friends go in there..

Ian: That's all you think of! What someone thinks of you! What impression you're making! That's so pathetic!

Mother: Look, this room had better be cleared up quickly! I want every single thing picked off the floor and put away properly. Not stuffed under the bed, mind you! Right away!

Ian: No! I said it's my room, and it's staying this way. Now, get out!

'This room had better be cleared up quickly! Right away!'

How many marks would you give them?

What's happening here? Perhaps you think Ian's point of view is reasonable enough - and maybe it is. But how many marks would you give either Ian or his mother for assertiveness? How many put downs can you count in that short conversation? Look at all the 'you-messages'. Can you sense the aggression, anger, and stubbornness between them? What effect do you think this way of treating each other has on their relationship?

And yet, this kind of behaviour happens a lot, doesn't it? Just ask yourself what *you* do when you don't get your own way. Attack the other person? Be nasty to everyone? Refuse to talk? Argue blindly? Refuse to listen?... Many of us have found our own ways of manipulating others or winning battles - but often at great cost. Issues like untidy bedrooms, lying in bed in the mornings, coming-in times in the evenings, household chores, and so on, can easily become battlefields where respect and friendship go out the window. Families suffer a great deal of unnecessary pain as a result, and relationships can become cold and empty.

And yet, passive, agreeable behaviour is hardly the answer. Going along, for the sake of 'peace', with what others want from you is equally unassertive. There is no respect for yourself in that approach.

I need to talk with you..

So what is the alternative? How can you deal with these thorny issues in an open, respectful way and still keep your own self-respect? Let's look now at how Ian might handle the bedroom issue more respectfully:

Mother: Ian, your room is an absolute mess! It's a disgrace! Really *disgusting*!

Ian: Look, I think we need to talk about this, Mum. This has been bothering you for a while now. Could we maybe talk about it when I come back from training this evening?

Mother: No, I want it cleared up now! Right away!

Ian: (sigh) Okay! I'm not going to fight with you. But I still need to talk. You okay for this evening?

Mother: I don't know what there is to talk about..

Ian: I *need* to talk with you. Please.

Mother: Oh, I'm not saying 'no.' I just don't know what there is to talk about.

Ian: Thanks.

Stage One - setting a time

That was stage one. Getting out of the heat of the moment and setting a time for talking. We cannot think clearly when we are angry or upset. Decisions are best made in a more relaxed atmosphere, when things are calmer. You may think Ian gave too much ground, even let himself be bossed around, but look at what happened. He had remained cool and respectful in spite of his mother's aggression and provocation. He had refused to take the bait, to waste his energy in an ineffective argument, and he had been effective in using 'I-messages' that expressed his needs. His mother may think she has 'won' that round, but Ian is not interested in 'winning' or in saving face - he has won the much more important battle of keeping the lines open. He is fighting for a respectful relationship, not for an empty victory.

You have a right to be involved in decisions that affect you. Sometimes that right is not respected, and you will need to ask for it. Ask for time to talk things through. Ask again - and again. Like Ian, say you *need* to talk about it. Keep asking until you're heard. That is part of being assertive.

I really didn't know..

Now let's see stage two. Later that evening, Ian and his mother sat down to talk.

Mother: (aggressively) Well, what is it? What do you want to say about your room?

Ian: I suppose the first thing I want to say is that I really don't think I understand what it is that bothers you so much about my room. I wonder... Maybe you'd explain, would you?..

Mother: What? It's obvious! Your room is a shambles! Dirty clothes, magazines, sheets of music, books, all scattered on the floor! There's hardly space to walk! And still you come in and dump your guitar on top of it all - then your football gear, even your muddy boots. And the smell! I don't know how you *breathe* in there!

Ian: (with some surprise in his voice) It really gets to you...

Mother: Of course it gets to me. What amazes me is that it doesn't get to *you*! Have you no self-respect! I would expect you at least to respect *yourself* if you can't respect the rest of us!

Ian: I didn't know it bothered you this much.

Mother: What do you mean you didn't know? I'm always on about your room!

Ian: Well, maybe I never took the time to sit down and listen to you about it before, but I really

'I need to talk with you.'

'Well, it is really. It's depressing..'

didn't know it was *so* annoying for you. I really didn't..

Mother: (softening) Well, now you know. I like to keep the house tidy. I've always kept a tidy house, and it just drives me up the wall to open the door of your room...

Ian: This seems to be... maybe... the thing that upsets you most about me...

Mother: Well, it is really. It's depressing..

Stage Two - Listening

How do you think Ian did in Round Two? Do you think he's giving too much ground? In the 'win-lose' type of world we live in, Ian may appear to be losing *all* the ground, but can you see what he's achieving?

We saw that the first stage of problem solving is to postpone dealing with the problem, not to attempt to deal with it in the heat of the moment. And now we see that the second stage is to begin the discussion, not by talking, not by presenting your own point of view, but, surprisingly, by listening. Ian's mother is unlikely to be able to hear his point of view until she has a chance to off-load some of the strong feelings, the exasperation, the annoyance, even her depression about the state of his room. Can you see how she softened when she realised her son was really listening to her? Genuine listening is a powerful start to problem solving. It's not easy. Ian, as we'll see, has his own strong feelings about the state of his room. He must have been quite anxious

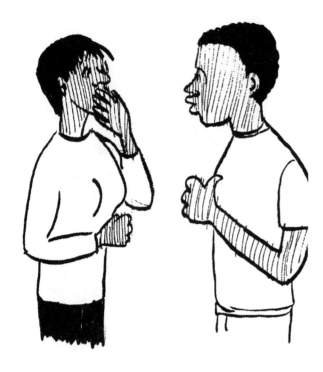

'No, I suppose I didn't know it meant so much to you..'

to have his own say. But this was the right start. Yet we mustn't see it as a mere technique. The goal is not to manipulate his mother. The listening needs to be so genuine that he opens himself up to hearing things that he'd rather not hear. That is obviously what had happened.

It is so helpful to start by listening. Most problem solving doesn't work because this crucial stage is left out. Ask questions. Listen well. Encourage the other to say more. Resist the temptation to argue. Check out that you've understood.

`Please don't interrupt'

Let's recap. Stage one, you have arranged a time when you can talk calmly. Stage two, you have listened well and given the other person a sense of being understood. Now it's time for stage three. Time for *you* to talk, to present *your* point of view.

Ian: Mum, I didn't know this was so depressing for you. I'd really like to make some changes. But before we move on to looking at what I can do, I'd like you to know first what it's like for me.

Mother: What do you mean?

Ian: Just what I say. I think I've a better understanding now of how you feel. But I need you to know how I feel about it all. Now, it may be hard for you to listen, but I'd really like you not to interrupt me until I've explained. Okay?

Mother: (reluctantly) Go ahead.

Ian: Well, it's like this. My room is the only place in the world that I feel is my space.

Mother: So why don't you keep it properly!

Ian: Hold on, Mum. You said you'd listen and let me have my say. I need you just to listen and try to understand. Please don't interrupt me until I finish. What I'm saying is that I feel I can be myself in my room. I can put things where I like..

Mother: But you do the same in the bathroom! You just drop your towel on the floor - *and* your dirty clothes..

Ian: Mum, please don't interrupt. If I sometimes drop things on the floor of the bathroom, I shouldn't, but can we talk about the bathroom another time?

Mother: No, I think it's all part of the same sloppy carelessness...

Ian: (sigh) Okay, we'll talk about that as well. But I'm feeling really frustrated now. You keep interrupting me. Will you please hear me out?..

Mother: Okay. I'm sorry.

Ian: Where was I?.. Oh yes, I feel I can be myself in my room. I can listen to my music. I can relax and be myself. I leave things where I like - I know it looks untidy, but I know where everything is. It's like my cave. Did you know it meant so much to me?

Mother: Well.. No. I suppose I didn't..

Ian: All I'm saying, then, is that, whatever plans we make, I need you to respect that my room is my space. It won't look like your room. It won't be just the way you'd like it.

Mother: You'll have to get rid of the smell! You can't just drop your dirty clothes on the floor!

Ian: Well, that's the kind of thing we need to talk about next...

Stage Three - Talking

Ian and his mother have now come to the end of stage three. Having first listened to her, he has now presented his own point of view, his feelings about having a room of his own, and his needs around that. It was like an extended I-message. That wasn't easy for him. His mother was difficult. She was a reluctant listener. She kept interrupting. He must have been tempted to throw in the towel at times, to tell her she was impossible, and to go off in a huff. Instead, he gave her another I-message. He told her how frustrated he was beginning to feel - and that did seem to help. In remaining flexible and keeping his cool, hanging in there in spite of his frustration, he was showing great maturity - and great assertiveness.

And that is the third stage of problem solving - saying how *you* feel, what *you* value, what *you* think, what *you* need. It is important to keep this balance between listening and speaking. The listening stage may be the most important one, but you mustn't become a doormat to others. You need to keep your dignity, to present *your* point of view. Otherwise, any 'solution' to a problem will be unbalanced.

'I want to paint my room black..'

At the end of the conversation above, it was obvious that Ian and his mother were ready to begin looking for solutions. That is the fourth stage in solving problems.

What is so different about this stage to what happens in everyday life? Maybe you'll see that for yourself as we listen to Ian and his mother talking:

Ian: I'd like us to put our heads together now to think up how each of us would like the room to be kept. Can we agree first that we'll not argue about any suggestions made?

Mother: Certainly. I don't want to argue with you.

Ian: Right. We're only thinking up possibilities. We'll not talk about them for a few minutes, until we've thought of as many as possible. So what solutions do you see?..

Mother: Well, it's simple. You just shape up! Have a place for things, and *keep* them in their place. That's all.

Ian: Hold on, I'd like to jot down the ideas we come up with. Otherwise, we'll forget. 'Have.. a.. place.. for.. things.' Any other ideas?

Mother: Yes. There should be nothing on your floor. Absolutely nothing!

Ian: (writing) 'Nothing.. on.. floor.'

It was difficult. His mother wanted it all her way. But Ian didn't react. He continued to jot down suggestions. Then he added in some of his own suggestions. To his mother's horror, these included: painting the walls of his room black; just leaving everything on the floor as it was but keeping the door shut so that she wouldn't have to look at the 'mess'; throwing out of his room the 'antique' chest of drawers granny had left to the family. When she reacted to these suggestions, he pointed out that they were only suggestions, and that they had agreed not to discuss them yet.

Stage Four - Any suggestions?..

Again, you can see Ian's maturity in not reacting to his mother's rigid 'solutions'. And that is what is so different about stage four of problem solving. With this kind of 'brainstorming', there is no arguing. Everything goes. Anything can be written down. In everyday life, there is a temptation to argue, to come in with an immediate, 'But...', to tear holes in each suggestion. That does not happen here. And that introduces great freedom into the process. Ideas tumble out that you might never have thought of. New possibilities begin to emerge. You may need to *experience* this to believe how effective it can be.

You don't *have* to write down the suggestions. In some families that may be too formal. But do consider it. It helps you to remember the different suggestions. And there is something very accepting about making a suggestion and seeing someone take it seriously enough to write it down instead of jumping down your throat or saying, 'That's stupid!'

Stage Five - good and bad effects

Next, stage five. You may be wondering now if all this isn't too time-consuming. It does take time. Maybe even twenty minutes or half an hour for the whole process. It's not something you'd want to do every day. But there's a lot to be said for talking things through and coming to new arrangements that respect both sides - instead of living with running battles that continue for years.

Ian and his mother began by going through the suggestions Ian had jotted down. For each one, they looked at the good and bad that might result. At times, this was difficult. For example, Ian's mother could see absolutely *no* good resulting from leaving things on the floor - until Ian pointed out that he had a huge need to do his own thing in at least *one* part of the house, without anyone nagging at him.

By the time they had gone though the list, they had a better understanding of each other, and it was obvious that some suggestions were out of the question. They were now readier to make decisions that might respect each other's needs. They understood that they would have to negotiate, that neither of them would get exactly what they wanted. They were ready for stage six.

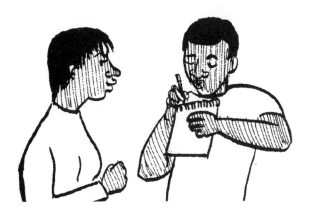

'I'll jot down the ideas.'

Stage Six - Decisions

And that is the final stage - making decisions. Ian and his mother were able to agree on the following details. 1. No *clothes* on the floor. 2. Keep door to his room shut at all times. 3. No more nagging about the state of his room. 4. They would sit down again, a week from Sunday, to see how the agreement was working out in practice. Ian wrote those decisions down so that they would have a record of what was decided, and there would be less chance of a dispute about it later.

He felt a sense of relief. There would be less nagging. Something important to him was going to be respected from now on. And his relationship with his mother had improved in the process. He was glad he had taken the initiative. He was fascinated, too, by these new skills he had learnt for dealing with conflict. They worked. Talking things out, one stage at a time, did help. These skills gave him power. Not power over others but over himself.. He began to see possibilities for dealing with thorny issues in different situations...

Two new skills

Can you begin to see how the six stages fit together and flow one into the other? 1. Timing - establishing the right atmosphere for talking. 2. Beginning by listening and understanding (for some personal problems, like having chosen the wrong career, the person you speak to is just a 'mentor', so this stage would be left out). 3. Saying how you see things, how you feel, and what you need. 4. Making suggestions, thinking up possibilities. 5. Looking at the advantages and disadvantages of these suggestions. 6. Making decisions - although the decisions made by Ian and his mother might not be at all suitable in *your* situation.

In previous chapters we have already met some of these helps to problem solving. But let's look now at stages four and five, for this is the first time we have come across these skills in this book. Here is a situation where they are being used.

What to do about a pregnancy?..

Kateri's best friend, Tara, is pregnant, and she has come to her, distressed, wondering what to do. In these circumstances, someone might need weeks (or months) of listening, so Kateri's support began with listening, for Tara desperately needed to talk - and to cry. Eventually, they began to look at possible solutions (with many problems it is not necessary to go down through all the different stages). Below are five possibilities that one or both of them thought up:

what to do about a pregnancy?...

How to look at the implications

You will notice that there are two columns beside the suggestions, for Tara and Kateri were now ready for stage five - it can be useful to draw a line down the middle of a page, making two separate columns for the good and bad consequences of each of the choices. Some of these suggestions may shock you, but problem solving is more effective when people are free to write down *all* suggestions, even some that one of you might not be open to. When people like Tara are in a highly emotional situation, it can be quite difficult for them to think straight, and they

POSSIBLE CHOICES	GOOD RESULTS	BAD RESULTS
1. Have baby adopted		
2. Abortion		
3. Tara's parents take baby		
4. Keep baby as lone parent		
5. Marry baby's father		

in a better position to make a decision

sometimes make decisions they later regret - just because they hadn't looked at the implications, the advantages and disadvantages, of the choices facing them.

Tara had been able to see some good results in *each* of the possibilities they had jotted down, including ways of giving maximum security to a future baby and greater freedom to herself. Then she looked at some bad results from the various choices, and ended up with a much wider picture and its implications. She was now in a better position to make a decision.

This was a big decision to have to make. It is best not to begin practising skills by tackling something that might be too ambitious or too discouraging. We have seen that new skills are best practised by starting with small, less important issues.

Why bother?

In this chapter, we have looked at how problems can be dealt with more effectively and more calmly when they are broken down and tackled in six separate stages. A framework like this will only be necessary for dealing with *some* problems. It is important to feel free to adapt it, to make it your own, to be flexible in how you use it. But you should see better decisions resulting from it. It is also much healthier to face up to conflict - neither attacking those who disagree with you nor running away from tensions. This would seem to be a more mature and more adult approach.

All through life, we have to deal with conflict - in families, at work, in the community, in marriage, in all our relationships. Yet these relationships can easily become sour, or cold, or they break down completely - just because people do not know how to communicate about problems and find 'no-lose solutions'. Good use of these skills, on the other hand, can do much to keep love and respect alive between people. A marriage, for example, can be exciting and alive when a couple learn to treat each other respectfully and solve their problems openly and fairly in this way. But there is no need to wait until we're 'older'. In the next twenty four hours, each of us will have opportunities to practise respectful problem solving. It *needs* to be practised. It will only gradually become *a way of life*. For that, as we hope to see in the next chapter, is the goal.

TABLE 7: SOLVING PROBLEMS

Here is a framework for solving problems - though you will only need to follow all six stages for some of the more serious problems you meet. Feel free to ignore some stages, to adapt the method, or to use your own way of saying things.

1. SET A TIME
It is hard to listen to each other in the heat of the moment. Set a time for talking when things are calmer.
'I need to talk with you. When can we have ten minutes to talk?..'

2. START WITH LISTENING
Most problem solving doesn't work because this crucial stage is left out. Start by listening. Ask questions. Resist the temptation to argue. Encourage the other to say more. Check out that you understand:
'Tell me first how you see things.. Mm.. Can you say a bit more about that?.. I see.. I wonder what makes you say that?.. Can you help me to understand this point better?.. How has all that left you feeling?.. I wonder now if I have grasped what you're saying - is it...?'

3. SAY WHAT <u>YOU</u> THINK AND FEEL
You have your point of view too. It's important to say what you think and feel.
'I've done my best to listen and understand - now I need you to understand my point of view. I know this may be difficult to listen to, but please hear me out without arguing... You see, I have a sense of.. I feel... Here's an example of what I'm talking about... Can you try to sum up what you hear me saying?..'

4. THINK OF POSSIBLE SOLUTIONS
Both of you - not just one of you - can think up suggestions for solving the problem. It may help to jot down ideas. Jot down any ideas, without discussing them, even things you're not open to.
'Let's think of some possibilities; we'll jot down *all* ideas first, and can we agree that there'll be no arguing or criticism of any suggestion at this stage? What might make both of us happier?... Any other ideas?... Good, any more?...'

5. LOOK AT GOOD AND BAD RESULTS
It may help to draw a line down the middle of a page, making two separate columns for the good and bad results. It's too easy to be critical - recognise the good as well as the bad in each idea.
'Right, let's look at the first suggestion. What do you see as the advantages there?.. Anything else?.. I see another advantage... Now the disadvantages. What are they?.. Any more?..'

6. DECISION TIME
In a joint decision both of you will not get exactly what you want. Be specific (who?, what? when? where? for how long?) Consider writing down what is decided - to avoid arguments later. Fix a time for looking at how things are working out in practice.
'Which solution seems to be best?.. Why do you say that?.. Are we being specific enough?.. What exactly will we do?.. When will you do that?.. Would you like to write down what we've decided?.. When will we look at how things are going?..'

GETTING IN TOUCH

Read briefly down through the examples below, and tick any that remind you of a situation that affects you. Form pairs and share your answers. How do you feel when you think about dealing with some of these issues more openly and assertively?

1. My sister has not been helping me with the chores as had been agreed.
2. I don't mind my room being untidy, but my brother/ sister who shares it is insisting I tidy it.
3. One of my friends is annoyed about something, and has stopped talking with me and my friends.
4. My boyfriend/girlfriend often turns up for a date much later than agreed and does not explain or apologise.
5. There is a lot of tension at home because I have stopped going to church and my parents are angry about that.
6. My father finds fault with me and nags a lot.
7. My brother embarrasses me by telling stories about me to my friends.
8. Unknown to my parents, I have begun drinking alcohol - I am sure they would disapprove.
9. My parents expect me to pay towards the household expenses now that I have a part-time job, but I'm not sure that's fair.
10. I regularly borrow my brother's/ sister's clothes without permission. This has led to a number of rows or 'scenes'.
11. My parents want to talk with me about staying out late.
12. My parents are annoyed that I lie on in bed on Saturday mornings/ come home so late/ watch so much TV.
13. Someone at work is picking on me and giving me a hard time.
14. Every morning, there is a queue for the bathroom, and I think it's unfair that my father skips the queue, saying he's the breadwinner and has to be at work on time.

CASE STUDIES

In the first column below, stage three of problem solving has been done - different possibilities have been written down for solving two problems. Choose either of the situations, or both, and take some time to look at the good and bad consequences of each of the possible choices.

A. Your friends want you to join them in smoking dope.

Possible choices	Good results	Bad results
1. Stay in group and smoke		
2. Stay in group but challenge		
3. Say 'no' but don't challenge		
4. Leave group but challenge them		
5. Leave group but don't challenge		
6. Leave group and inform someone.		
7. Another choice?...		

B. You've chosen what seems like the wrong subject or course (or career)

Possible choices	Good results	Bad results
1. Take extra tuition		
2. Change school or college		
3. Drop out of education		
4. See about changing courses		
5. Go back and repeat year		
6. Get job, but take night classes.		
7. Do nothing about it		

SKILL PRACTICE

Form groups of three. Choose a problem from the Getting in Touch section - or, better still, from your own life - and try going down through the different stages in Table 7, dealing with it. Don't tackle anything too ambitious or too discouraging - it is best to start with small, less important issues. A second person in the group will be the person to whom you need to talk about the problem. The third person is the observer. After attempting to solve the problem, chat about what you learned before switching to a second situation and changing roles.

PLANNING FOR NEXT WEEK

Please read chapter eight for next week - it helps to have the chapter read before each session.

During the next week, it is suggested that you practise being assertive at least once each day, but that you might also set up an actual six-stage problem-solving session about one problem you would like to deal with, perhaps in your own family.

1. What problem would you like to deal with?
2. When do you think you will need to be assertive in the next 24 hours or so?

Plans... _____

_____

CHAPTER EIGHT: A WAY OF LIFE

Jenny felt frustrated, even suffocated, by her parents. They were *so* protective. They decided what television she watched. They planned her study time. They wanted her in before ten - even at weekends. She was almost eighteen now, but she felt she could do nothing without consulting them. It almost seemed as if they wanted to make all her decisions for her. Worst of all, they would not listen when she protested. She had tried talking with them time and again, but they kept saying that she didn't know the dangers. Somehow, they just could not hear her frustration. How could she make them hear?

'I am very unhappy at home.'

She considered a hunger-strike! - 'A bit drastic,' she thought, 'Maybe as a last straw...'

Another possibility was to give her parents a shock - move in with her aunt until they listened to her. She didn't rule that out either, but she preferred something less upsetting - provided it would work.

Eventually, she decided to write them a letter. She felt there was a better chance of them hearing what she had to say if she wrote it down. Here is what she wrote:

'Dear Mum and Dad...'

'Dear Mum and Dad, I'm sure you'll be surprised to get a letter from me, but I don't know any other way of getting you to listen. I have tried again and again to talk with you, and I just seemed to get nowhere.'

'I am very unhappy at home. Very unhappy. I know that you are both doing your best, and that you mean well. I know you want to protect me from dangers that you think I am unaware of. Indeed, I'm sure I'm not aware of all the dangers. But equally, I don't think you're aware of how frustrated and hemmed in I feel. I am not allowed anything like the freedom my friends enjoy. I feel terribly tied in deciding where to go, when to go out, who to go out with, and what time to be back home. It's awful. I want to be able to make my own decisions, even to make my own mistakes. I need you to treat me as someone who is becoming an adult. If you don't let me take more responsibility for myself and let me make my own decisions, how do you think I'm going to cope in a year's time when I'll be living away from home?'

'I'm not asking for complete freedom. But please don't read this letter and start talking to me again about the dangers and about the need to protect me from myself. If you do, this letter will have been a waste of time. I need you to hear that I'm unhappy and that I need you to treat me as someone who is not a child any longer. Your loving daughter, Jenny.'

frustrated by her parents

Taking action

The effect of that letter was quite dramatic. Her parents were shocked. A little defensive, yes, but they heard loud and clear what they had failed to hear before. For the first time, they took their daughter seriously. Naturally, they didn't let go of the controls completely, but Jenny experienced a different atmosphere at home from then on.

What was it that had made the difference? Wasn't it that Jenny had taken *action*? Very often, a gentle, low-key approach is all that is needed - a simple I-message may be enough to correct something annoying. But sometimes talking is not enough. Sometimes action is called for. Jenny had considered a number of different kinds of action and had opted for writing a letter as the least upsetting one. Because assertiveness is so respectful, it is recommended that we try a less upsetting approach first and only gradually consider something tougher.

...what they had failed to hear..

Do you enjoy life?

Assertiveness, then, properly understood, is not just about communicating. It includes taking action. It is not just a set of communication skills. It is a whole way of life, a way of looking at things, a way of living. It encourages us to be more open and free in the way we live. It gives us the freedom not to let ourselves be cramped by aggressive habits, nor by fears of what others might think. It frees us to *enjoy* life.

Assertiveness *invites* us to enjoy it, to stop drifting along, existing, merely coping. It invites us to take greater control of our lives, to move out of the ruts we may have got into, and to be at peace with ourselves. Maybe that means getting out more often to a park or the countryside. Maybe it's a question of joining a club or organisation - for exercise, or for a better social life, or to help others who are less well off. Or you may want to develop yourself, to read more, to be well informed, to meditate, or to learn a musical instrument. There is a list of things you may like to do - or stop doing. - in the Planning section at the end of this chapter. You can never do all the things you'd like to do, but it may be a good idea to look over that list from time to time and to ask yourself how you're looking after yourself, relaxing, improving yourself, even risking and stretching yourself a little.

Keeping a balance

Now, this emphasis on self can easily be misunderstood. Obviously it has to be balanced. It doesn't mean doing everything you *feel* like doing. Feelings are poor decision makers. We have seen how easily friendships, marriages, families, any relationships, can break down when we act on feelings. If it is true that love is more a *decision* than a feeling, then people who simply act on feelings, opt in and out of relationships, and 'do their own thing' would seem to be missing the point.

It's not easy to find the balance between loving others and loving ourselves, between caring about *my* needs and caring about *your* needs. If I bury my feelings, smile, and concentrate on *your* needs, I am losing the balance; I am doing violence to myself. Equally, if I concentrate on getting *my* rights, and claiming *my* space, and doing things *I* enjoy, I am still losing the balance - it is that kind of misunderstanding that gives 'assertiveness' a bad name. We have seen that being assertive includes being willing to do a certain amount of negotiating and settling for *less* than I might want, because I respect your rights as well as my own.

That may be difficult to accept. When we were children we were dependent. As we grew older, independence felt good. That was an important stage. But psychologists tell us independence is *only* a stage on the way to real maturity and adulthood. The true goal, they say, is not independence, but *inter*dependence - balancing our own needs and those of others, co-operating, communicating, pulling together, team-work...

Real maturity

It is particularly difficult to practise this co-operation and communication with those who live closest to us. Perhaps that is the biggest challenge of assertiveness. There is a strong temptation to walk away when things become difficult. Or there is always the temptation to settle for a surface relationship - not to talk, especially not to talk on the feeling level - rather than risk conflict with parents or guardians, with friends, with a sister or brother. People are even praised in our society for 'keeping the peace' with this kind of fear and unwillingness to face tensions.

It is not easy to face tensions, to work at a relationship, to stay in there, and listen, and share your feelings, and negotiate, and work for change, with someone who is very different to you. Independence is a lot more attractive than interdependence in the short term. It is easier to go it alone, to opt out of a relationship, or just leave things the way they are, than to hang in there and work alongside others for change in your family, in your community, in your church or other organisation - or in any relationships you may form in the future.

Practising with small things

It is not unusual to hear young adults say that they want to have better marriages and better relationships in the future than the ones they see around them today. In a group recently, one teenager saw so much that was wrong with his father's approach that he said he was actually looking forward to having his own family and helping them through the teenage years - he would do things differently. But how different will he be? *Now* is the time to start, to practise, to listen to those close to you, to share needs and feelings, to begin to face tensions. Every single day you have opportunities to practise treating family members with respect. You may be leaving home soon, and perhaps you think it's not worth investing the time in a family that may now be less and less important to you than your friends. But how else will you learn? How else will you practise?..

Do remember, though, to start practising with small things, where you can get a taste of success. Those who teach assertiveness recommend that you concentrate on one skill, or on one part of a skill, at a time. You may want to become a more positive person, for example, but it may be enough, for a start, to try cutting out critical or hurtful remarks, to hold your tongue, not to correct people without thinking. Or maybe you'd prefer to concentrate on developing the habit of speaking more honestly and openly to your friends and family about yourself and your feelings. Or to practise listening and giving

'I would like you not to smoke in here'

people a sense of being understood. No one is a better judge of where to start than yourself.

The key word is 'respect'

It is all the more important to start small when there is a such a *variety* of different skills involved in being assertive - making requests, dealing with requests from others, expressing your needs, feelings, ideas, giving constructive criticism, dealing with criticism that is directed at you, listening, problem solving, giving compliments, receiving compliments - and now taking action! In this last chapter, it may be useful, to take some time to look at what it is that ties together such different skills under one heading. That may help us to understand assertiveness better.

Perhaps the key word is respect. Respect for yourself and for others. That is why aggressive behaviour (which does not respect others) is not assertive. That is why passive, oppressed behaviour (which does not respect yourself) is not assertive either. Assertiveness is all about respect, and it shows itself in communication and behaviour that is increasingly open and free.

Open about yourself

That word 'open' seems to be crucial. Being more direct and honest and open in how you express yourself, without aggression or apology. Open in expressing your feelings, 'I'm in bad form today'; 'I feel sad when you talk to her like that.' Open in expressing your needs, 'I need time to think about this.' 'I need a rest.' Open with your requests, 'I would like you not to smoke in here' 'Will you repeat those instructions again please.' Open about your beliefs and opinions, 'I believe that sex is something too intimate for people who don't know each other well.' 'I support the Labour Party.' 'I think capital punishment is right/wrong.' This openness is not just about your negative opinions and feelings, but about your positive ones too, so it includes compliments: 'I'm impressed at how well you've done that.' 'I like the calm way you corrected him.'

It is not always appropriate to speak personally. Even when it is, it may involve taking a risk, particularly when your beliefs or ideas are unpopular, or when others might judge you on your feelings. That can take courage.

Open to requests or criticisms

Assertiveness also encourages you to be thoughtful and open when you meet with problems, requests, demands, or criticisms - instead of passively accepting criticisms, or agreeing to requests out of weakness - or reacting aggressively.

You begin with an openness to listening, perhaps asking questions: 'Why did you call me that?' 'How long do you want to borrow it for?' 'Why do you say that I'm unfair?' Then, if you need time, you can say so, for that is one of your rights, 'I'll need time to think this over.' 'I'll come back to you when I've had a chance to consider it.' When you do come back, you may need to present your own viewpoint and feelings, and to be open to negotiating a little, 'I wonder how we can meet each other's needs in this situation?..' Your response then can be a clear, direct acceptance or agreement - or a firm but gentle refusal or denial, 'Okay, I'm happy to give it a try.' 'No, I'm not responsible for the mistake.'

A 'no' will not always be accepted respectfully,

How long do you want to borrow it for?'

when a member of your family goes off in a huff

so you may then need to use 'broken record' firmly and calmly, 'Yes, I can hear what you're saying, but I'm not responsible for the mistake...'

Openness in criticising or confronting

Openness is also helpful when you need to correct or challenge someone's behaviour. It is important to be specific in pointing out what is wrong, but the correction will come across much more powerfully when you also say openly how that behaviour makes you feel, 'That's the second time you haven't turned up - after promising that you would be here - and I feel so frustrated that I don't know where to go from here. Only I want to be friends with you I wouldn't bother telling you this.' Or, 'I was angry that you shouted at me. What hurt me most was that Tom was listening - I felt so humiliated. I know you didn't do it deliberately, but I need you to know how hurtful it was.'

You notice the positive ending in each case. An 'I-message' is much more effective when you include something positive. This positive note is best towards the end of a correction, but that is not a cast-iron rule - the letter at the beginning of this chapter was a kind of correction, wasn't it, and it included some positive, understanding comments that did not come at the end.

Respect breeds respect

The effect of treating others with respect and openness has to be experienced to be believed. For, just as aggression breeds aggression, respect breeds respect. You change the atmosphere in your home when you show respect. Your friendships become more real and satisfying. Assertive skills also cut through the pretences and barriers that destroy relationships. Take, for example, a common form of non-communication - when a friend or a member of your family goes off in a huff, avoids you, or refuses to talk. Perhaps you need to let some cooling down time go by first, as they probably feel misunderstood and angry. Then you move in, not to confront them with indignation ('What **is** wrong with you!' 'When are you going to stop being so immature!') but with respect and openness. It may not help to say, 'We need to talk!' That could be off-putting or threatening. Better to be open and personal, using 'I' rather than 'we' - 'I'd like a chat.' That may be all that is needed. If they hedge, or are not co-operative ('There's no point in talking any more!'), you can then make a stronger statement, but keep it personal - you might say, 'I *need* a chat with you.' Your openness and directness will usually break down the resistance. If that doesn't work, you may just need to respect their right not to talk, or you say, 'When you want to talk, I'm here.' Respect is what it's all about.

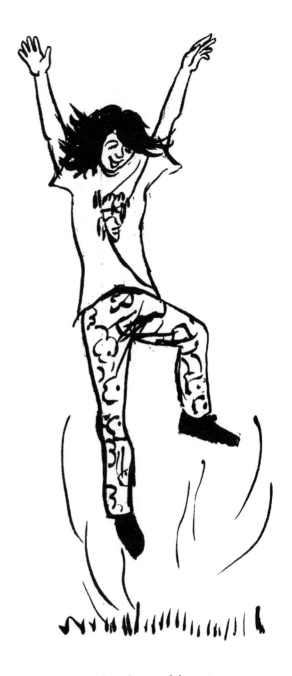

...to break out of the rut

someone with whom you can sit down to talk out and then role-play

Will I be different?

But don't let yourself get discouraged if you read this and think, 'When I read these examples, I nod my head, and I'd love to be more assertive, but I'm never able to think of the right things to say. In an everyday situation, I'm a million miles away from that!'

That's perfectly normal. At the end of an assertiveness course, you are only beginning. But the difference lies in your *awareness*. You are more aware of assertiveness now, of what it is and what it isn't. Awareness is the first step in making a change. Indeed, it is strongly recommended that you take some time each evening to become aware of how you have used (and failed to use) assertive skills that day. That daily awareness may not bring immediate change, but it can be remarkably effective over a period of time.

Another thing that can help a lot is to find someone with whom you can sit down to talk out and then role-play before any difficult situation you have to deal with - before a job interview, before a meeting with someone who tends to be aggressive, before confronting someone in your family. Practise dealing with the situation a number of times, getting feedback each time until you know you are coming across assertively. That will normally give you greater confidence in dealing with a situation.

Discover your own power

The invitation, then, is to break out of the ruts you may be in and to take charge of your life, to enjoy your family, your friends, your work, your leisure, yourself - and to help others to enjoy life. Assertiveness enables you to do that. Begin by taking small risks. Stop listening to old whispers in your ear about things being hopeless - contradict them. Plan a bit more. Begin to break that addiction - to always trying to win the approval of your friends, to finding fault, to whatever. Addictions do violence to you and limit your freedom. Stop waiting for things to happen - take the initiative. Face up to a problem in your life. Plan to do something you'll enjoy. Ask your parents to read this book. Tell someone who is abusing your rights that you need to talk with them. Discover your own power and freedom and self-respect, and your life will become more fulfilling, more reflective and more rewarding.

Do you believe the world can be a more just and peaceful place? If you do, it's hardly a good idea to wade in angrily to try and change things. Peace begins with you. It is a fundamental belief of those who teach assertiveness that **you cannot change others; you can only change yourself.** And perhaps the most important change you will ever make is self-acceptance - accepting that you'll never be perfect, that you may not even be able to change very much, that you'll always have to live with your imperfect self and your imperfect family or friends. When you begin to accept that, you may find peace - and that peace may begin to change things, because your family and friends will learn about peace and respect and acceptance more effectively when they experience you as peaceful and respectful and accepting. That's all part of the invitation to be assertive.

TABLE 8: ASSERTIVE SKILLS

This is a summary of the principal assertive skills that we have met during the course. They are under four main headings, but these divisions are not rigid - if someone is hostile, for example, approaches two or three may be appropriate. Where do you think you have improved, and where do you still tend to be too aggressive or too passive?

---

1. OPENLY EXPRESSING OPINIONS, FEELINGS, NEEDS, COMPLIMENTS
- BE BRIEF, DIRECT, CLEAR, AND SPECIFIC
- SPEAK PERSONALLY
- LOOK DIRECTLY AT THE PERSON, STAY CALM, NO APOLOGY

---

2. DEALING OPENLY WITH REQUESTS OR CRITICISM
- ASK OPEN QUESTIONS
- ASK FOR TIME, IF NECESSARY
- THEN GIVE YOUR RESPONSE DIRECTLY, FIRMLY, GENTLY
- USE 'BROKEN RECORD' IF YOU'RE NOT BEING RESPECTED

---

3. OPENLY GIVING CRITICISM
- GIVE A CLEAR EXAMPLE OF THE BEHAVIOUR
- MENTION THE EFFECT (INCLUDING THE EFFECT ON YOUR FEELINGS)
- END WITH A SPECIFIC SINCERE COMPLIMENT, IF POSSIBLE

---

4. SOLVING PROBLEMS
- BEGIN BY LISTENING
- PRESENT YOUR POINT OF VIEW (THOUGHTS, FEELINGS, NEEDS..)
- THINK UP POSSIBLE SOLUTIONS
- CHOOSE A SOLUTION AND PLAN THE DETAILS

GETTING IN TOUCH

Take a minute or so to read down through the list below, and put a tick beside any examples that remind you of situations in your own life that you'd like to deal with assertively. Then, form groups of three and take a few minutes to talk together about some of these situations.

1. EXPRESSING OPINIONS, FEELINGS, NEEDS, REQUESTS, COMPLIMENTS..

* You want to ask your parents for more money.
* You want to change a course/subject at school or university - or to change your job.
* You don't understand what your new employer is asking you to do, but you're afraid of appearing stupid if you ask.
* You'd like to have a regular chat with your parent(s)/ guardians, when they would really listen to anything you want to talk about, including how you'd like to be treated.
* You'd like to compliment someone on something you've noticed. How will you express it?

2. DEALING WITH REQUESTS OR CRITICISM

* Your older brother asks for a loan of your new sweater and he won't take 'no' for an answer.
* An insensitive friend says your hair looks awful.
* Your father says you've no sense of responsibility.
* Your supervisor asks you to work overtime, but you've a date.
* Your mother wants you to help with the chores - and to pay her half of what you earn now that you have a part-time job.

3. GIVING CONSTRUCTIVE CRITICISM/ CONFRONTING

* You'd like to do something about someone who is constantly correcting you in an aggressive tone of voice.
* The people behind you in the cinema are quite noisy.
* Your father makes it obvious that your sister is his 'pet'.
* A friend is quite nosey and asks you personal questions.
* The friends you hang around with make sexist remarks. Since doing the course, you're aware now of how unfair that is.
* You want to return a pair of shoes because they are leaking.

4. SOLVING PROBLEMS (Be open to giving some ground.)

* Your parents want you to come on holidays with them as usual, but you want to go with your friends.
* Tension has arisen between you and your friend because of a misunderstanding. (S)he has avoided you for the past few days.
* You end up doing an unfair proportion of the chores at home. You want everyone to do a fair share.
* You find smoking offensive but don't want to hurt the feelings of a friend who smokes a lot.
* Your parents are quite strict about 'suitable' television programmes, and you'd like to talk it out with them.
* There's constant squabbling about which TV channel to watch.

CASE STUDIES/ SKILL PRACTICE

Remain in the group of three. Choose a situation from the list below - or one that you'd like to deal with assertively (but not something big like standing up to an authoritarian figure). Decide who you will work with, and who the observer will be.

Before acting it out, you may like to talk briefly about the approach you will take, consulting Table 8 for ideas, if necessary. Before moving on to another situation and switching roles, take time for feedback from your 'observer'.

PLANNING FOR THE FUTURE

Below is a list of things you may like to do. As you read through it, tick anything you would enjoy doing. Add to the list if you like. Then underline two things you'd like to do more regularly. What will you do about one of them in the next 48 hours?

When you have ticked the list, and planned, talk in pairs about what you would like to do, what prevents you from doing it, how you could be assertive in this area, and what might help you to keep going. Help each other to write down one definite plan.

Take a rest in the evening.
Go for a walk more often - somewhere you like.
Read a good novel - or a book about something that interests you.
Go for cycle rides.
More dancing.
Read a magazine/ newspaper.
Swim regularly.
Listen to music.
Play indoor/ outdoor games of......
Enjoy a bath/ shower more often.
Meditate.
Take a part-time job.
Learn a new skill/ musical instrument/ language......
Plan more effective ways of studying.
Ask your parent(s)/ guardians for an evening in the week to chat about decisions that affect you, perhaps over a special supper.
Make a new friend.
Join a keep-fit class.
Practise relaxation methods regularly (like deep breathing).
Cut out critical or hurtful remarks and become a more positive person.
Re-read this book, a chapter a week, and work on the corresponding skills for that week.
Plan a new career or job.

Plans... _____

_____

FEEDBACK

These comments were made by young adults who had experienced the course

We need to hear this stuff. The reason we act tough and aggressive is because we didn't know there was an alternative. It's good to even know that there is a different way.

As the only girl in my family, I'm an easy target for my brothers. There is such a constant attack on my appearance, the spots on my face, my weight, and so on, that it really gets to me at times and I end up believing the worst about myself.

No. I mean, if someone called me an idiot, I would just tell her to shut up, or I'd fight back and tell her she was a bigger idiot. That's what everyone does.

I went for a walk with my friend, and I really did listen well to her. I know she noticed the difference, because, when she was leaving me, she looked at me differently and she said `Thanks for everything'.

You read the examples in the book and think 'That's dead obvious' but then you realise you don't act like that yourself. It makes you think.

I have often gone off in a huff, even kept up the silence with my parents for a few days, and I enjoyed the feeling of power I got from 'punishing' them like that - I didn't care about the atmosphere I created. But it was no way to deal with conflict. It was childish. I needed this course to help me to grow up.

I found the style of the book a bit preachy and condescending at times. Just in parts, but you have to be very careful of that. Young people don't need another adult talking down to them about how we should live. I get enough of that.

I've learnt how to be a better person, to think before I react, and to approach people more confidently. I feel 'sorted'!

The way the other boys talk about girls is terrible. I hate it. But it's too difficult to be different - I do it too.

This course is a 'yes'! Good fun. A chance to meet new people who are now great friends. Real topics. And people listen to what you have to say. It teaches you a lot.

GROUNDRULES

Those taking part in the programme tend to feel safer when the following Groundrules are agreed right from the start.

1. Take it seriously You are asked to practise the skills at least once each day during the course, and to take some time each evening a) to become aware of how you've been doing, and b) to imagine yourself acting assertively in a situation you'll meet the following day. Regular practice between sessions is the key to the success of the programme.

2. No pressure You have a right not to speak, and that right will always be respected. Nor will you ever be forced to do anything in front of the group that you don't want to do.

3. Encourage others to speak One of the best ways of encouraging others to speak is to listen with good attention, and certainly not to talk or giggle while others are talking, nor to laugh at what anyone says. You are also asked to draw others out and encourage them to talk first. This ground rule is particularly important for males; it is not uncommon for men to take over and do most of the talking in mixed groups.

4. Respect people's confidences It is *very* important to respect people's trust and not to talk with anyone else about what you hear in the group.

5. Start small Don't start by tackling very difficult situations or making major decisions. Better to build up your confidence by practising assertiveness in easier, simple situations first. Starting small also means starting with yourself. Do not attempt to change your friends, your parents or teachers, your brothers or sisters - they will only begin to change when you do.

6. Beat discouragement As you improve, you will sometimes have a bad day when you seem to go backwards. That is normal - everyone has off-days. Don't let yourself become discouraged or think you have failed if you are slow about changing the habits of a lifetime.

7. No preaching The input for this course comes from the video and from the handbook - not from the leaders. So no one will be telling you how to behave or giving you advice. But please show the same respect to the others in the group. They all have a right to their own approach and their own pace. What works for you may not work for them, so feel free to say what works for you, but please don't offer advice to others or put any pressure on others to change.

8. Question all put downs You are asked to encourage and support each other in becoming more assertive. Also to support your group presenter by questioning any racist, sexist, or other remark that appears to put down any person or group of people.

9. Anything else... that would help you feel safer in the group?